THE

AGE

OF

ALIENATION

also by Bernard Murchland

The Meaning of the Death of God (editor)

THE

AGE

OF

ALIENATION

Bernard Murchland

Random House : New York

Some materials from Part II originally appeared in *Buffalo Studies* and portions of Part III were first published in *worldview*. They are used here with permission.

"The Peace of Wild Things," by Wendell Berry, is reprinted from his volume *Openings*, by permission of Harcourt, Brace, Javanovich, Inc. Copyright (C) 1968 by Wendell Berry.

For Joan

All burrowing into existence consists in establishing connections.
—S. Kierkegaard

The net effect of the establishment of a boundary between self and the external world is inside-out and outside-in: confusion. The erection of a boundary does not alter the fact that there is, in reality, no boundary. The net-effect is illusion: the big lie. Or alienation.
—Norman O. Brown

The true mystery of the world is the visible, not the invisible.
—Oscar Wilde

Everyone is more or less sick of the plague.
—Albert Camus

Preface

We seem indisputably to be living through one of those periods of cultural collapse that periodically overtake history, a time when the human estate is at low ebb, only tenuously connected to the sources of its replenishment. We live, as it has become fashionable to say, under the dispensation of alienation. Alienation is indeed a term of the first importance in our lexicon of cultural criticism.

It is also, as one would expect, a complex term. No one study can hope to be more than explorative and tentative. This is particularly true of my own study. The first level of complexity concerns the different shades of meaning the word "alienation" has in contemporary usages. Sorting these out, analyzing their content and relating them one to the other constitute an immense critical task. Secondly, the intellectual antecedents of the modern phenomenon of alienation run deep. I have rather stressed this aspect of the problem in the following essay because, quite apart from being a neglected aspect, it reveals something important about man's historical being. It has become clear to me that many of our present dilemmas originate in the uses to which reason has been put in the course of history. To say that our roots are in the past is to say among other things that we have inherited a cluster of ideas, values and attitudes that are in essence alienative. Effective social criticism today, therefore, must include an analysis of received beliefs in light of their origins. Critical thinking functions in one of its most useful modes when it clarifies our social reality through an examination of the key concepts of our cultural tradition. Taking this as a guiding principle, I have tried to show that an ideology of alienation lies close to the heart of Western man's principal cultural expressions. This ideology has been transmitted to us and forms part and parcel of what has been quite appropriately called the exhausting logic of modern life.

But I do not want to exaggerate the historical aspect of the problem. The benefits of history are always to some extent dubious, even as our understanding of it is partial. A far more crucial question is how alienation is to be overcome. There is, of course, no way of answering this question satisfactorily, for the simple reason that no one knows the future. Our present predicament stirs our curiosity but it cannot settle our doubt in this regard. To be modern is to be a castle seeker, to quest more than to find. But even here, history provides a clue by furnishing us with the record of man's survival ability. Man has always survived his major cultural crises because of his resourcefulness, his imagination, his creativity. He has survived, in a word, because of his genius for inventing suitable myths. Myth, in this strong sense of the word, I understand to be those shared experiences which give cohesion and purpose to our social institutions and sustain our value patterns. For example, after the collapse of the Roman empire, man developed a religion; after the Copernican revolution, a science; after Darwin, progress. And so forth. The myths of the past are rarely serviceable in our present situation, at least not without serious adaptation. More often, in fact, past solutions are present problems. But the historical record does suggest that an answer is to be found in redirecting our creative energies. I explore this line of thought briefly in the final section of my book and conclude that our hope lies in some effective combination of art and politics.

I have been influenced by many sources and thinkers and make a conscious effort to acknowledge them in my notes. But I have no doubt in some cases assimilated the ideas of others so completely that they are indistinguishable from my own. To all I am grateful.

I particularly wish to thank Professor John Anton, chairman of the philosophy department at Emory University. His sound advice and constant encouragement had much to do with the book's genesis. I am indebted to my colleagues at Ohio Wesleyan University. I have learned much from them. Dr. Loyd Easton read parts of the manuscript and made valuable comments. A special thanks to Alice Mayhew for indispensable editorial guidance and all at Random House who have lent assistance.

Contents

Part III

THE END of ALIENATION?

Part I

MAN
IN ESTRANGE-
MENT

It can be convincingly argued that alienation is central to contemporary speculation about man and his place in the world. Wherever the search for an understanding of the human condition is going on today, the notions of alienation and cultural disintegration are indispensable. In a passage that has assumed near-classic status, C. W. Mills has said: "The advent of the alienated man and all the themes which lie behind his advent now affect the whole of our serious intellectual life and cause our immediate intellectual malaise." The malaise, it might be added, is not merely an intellectual one. It is much more widespread, penetrating to all levels of our awareness and coloring all of our interests and concern.

Consider the following quotations:

► The sixties were a decade of discontinuities, by which I mean violent breaks in the flow of history. They came in almost every vital area of society.

► It was a decade in which simple intellectual honesty compelled us to face up to the strong possibility that we humans are just about at the end of our days.

► At this point, hate and love seem to be merging into a sense of cosmic failure, a pervasive feeling that everything is disintegrating, including the counter-culture itself, and that we really have nowhere to go.

► We live in an expanding theater of the absurd and the unreal.

► We see ourselves diminished, puttering, dispirited, destroyed, numbered, computerized, propagandized, spied on, tapped, hounded, busted, lobotomized, big-brothered to smithereens.

□ THE AGE OF ALIENATION

► Man's greatest challenge in the 1970's is to find a reason for his own existence.

► One turns the pages of the daily newspapers in vain search for some shred of agreement, reconciliation, continuity. But the reports are reports of a people who are at worst mean-tempered and at best vaguely uneasy about distant forces over which they exercise diminishing control.

► It is no longer possible to say to young people that this is a benevolent or trustworthy or even in any reasonable degree sane society.

These are random samplings of opinion as one decade ends and another begins. The theme in all of them is alienation. They typically express our present discontents, unrelieved by any proportionate hope for future resolution. Our society is so complex and frightening and solutions so difficult to come by that a kind of general paralysis of will (a moral paralysis, I would call it) has descended upon us. Alienation emerges as the inclusive category which points to our personal and social frustrations, to our sense of collapse and doom and to the critical nature of the human situation at this juncture in history. When we turn to the vast body of literature on the subject we are informed that in various ways novels, poetry, drama, art, theology and philosophy are centrally preoccupied with alienation—a term used broadly to include such multiple disorders as loss of self, anxiety states, anomie, despair, depersonalization, rootlessness, meaninglessness, isolation, pessimism and lack of community. We are said to be alienated from nature, our past, God, society and its institutions, work, friends and neighbors, values, our emotions and sexuality, the environment and in the end ourselves. This condition is obvious in some segments of our society—among the poor, blacks, women, students, industrial workers, the mentally ill, the aged, dope addicts, etc. It is perhaps less obvious but equally destructive at all levels of society—among voters, consumers, middle Americans, all of us. The term, clearly, suffers from generality. It says, as it were, too much. As one critic has put it: "In current literature it is often difficult to differentiate alienation and dyspepsia."[1]

The Metaphors of Disconnection

Such descriptive generality, however, is not very useful when applied to a concept like alienation. Perhaps we can profitably begin to focus it by considering some of the ways in which it has been handled in creative literature. In general, it is considered to be some form of disconnection in the pattern of experience, a disrelationship between the self and its world. Kafka's *The Castle* is an excellent expression of alienation understood in this way.* It deals powerfully with one man's inability to cope with his society and fellow-man, his failure to achieve a satisfactory measure of self-realization, his ignorance of the conditions under which his life might have been happy. The novel's hero, K., enters an isolated village late one winter evening. This village is to be his world, the locus of his struggle and eventual failure. As he approaches he stands for a long time gazing into "the illusory emptiness above him," where the Castle is shrouded in darkness. From the outset we suspect that the goal he has set for himself is an impossible one. As Martin Greenberg observes: "When K. turns off the main road and crosses the

---

* I do not mean to imply that so rich and complex a novel can be reduced to a sociological critique. But whatever else it may be, it is at least a vivid portrayal of social alienation.

bridge into the village, he leaves behind the ordinary world, warm with its densely packed humanity and wholly preoccupied with the business of living, and arrives at a solitary freezing outpost of the human spirit, a lonely, ultimate frontier."[2] Thus does K. emerge nameless from an unknown past to face a problematic future. His daily life will be defined by an exhausting effort to forge some connection with the values of normal existence. He will attempt to exercise his profession, to communicate, to enjoy, to love—in a word, to live. But the path to fulfillment is beset with insurmountable obstacles; authentic existence is never more than dimly perceived at a great distance in the future. This reflection from one of Kafka's letters might aptly be applied to K.: "I am separated from all things by a hollow space."

What K. is primarily separated from, of course, is the Castle itself, which is the primary symbol of alienation in the novel, the goal that does not and cannot enrich. The Castle is, at the most obvious level, a stifling bureaucracy, complete with repressive authority, jammed channels of communication and a hierarchy of officials, working overtime and producing nothing but a mountain of forms and files, who indulge in sordid pleasures on their time off. We recognize in the Castle the familiar features of modern society where, as Austin Warren writes nicely, one is forever being orally examined by dignitaries who forever flunk one. In this world, calls are never returned, petitions always reach the wrong official, relevant documents are lost, so that things finally become so muddled that even the simplest requirements of justice cannot be met. It is, quite simply, a nightmarish world with which the self is forever juxtaposed in opposition. K.'s first rude encounter with this world comes shortly after he has gone to sleep on the night of his arrival in the village. He is awakened by a minor official who informs him he cannot sleep there without permission from the Castle. And since he cannot get a permit in the middle of the night, he is ordered to leave. K. explains that he is in the employ of the Castle, that he has come to be the land-surveyor. After a series of misunderstandings, against the grotesque backdrop of the tavern, a phone call seems to confirm that this is the case, and for the moment K. is left in peace. A serious threat to his identity has already been posed, however, and for the rest of the novel he will never relax his efforts to confirm his appointment. In so striving he never gets a clear grasp of the boundary line between appearance and reality, truth and illusion, the fantastic and the normal.

His first day in the village dawns bright and clear and he sets out to settle matters with the officials. "He could see the Castle above him, clearly defined in the glittering air, its outline made still more definite by the thin layer of snow covering everything." It seemed readily accessible. Yet here as everywhere in the novel appearances are deceptive. "But the way proved long. For the street he was in, the main street of the village, did not lead up to the Castle hill; it only made toward it and then, as if deliberately, turned aside, and though it did not lead away from the Castle, it led no nearer it either. At every turn K. expected the road to double back to the Castle." It never did. K. ends up in a maze of snow-filled side streets, so fatigued that "he could not go on." It is already dark and he cannot account for the swift passage of time. "Short days, short days," he reflects. He has begun to experience that distortion of time and space that reflects the deeper malady of his psyche. When he returns to the inn he finds that he has been assigned two assistants who are "as alike as two snakes." This seems further confirmation of his appointment, especially since a messenger soon delivers a letter telling him that "he has been engaged in the Count's service" and that he is to report to the Mayor for specific instructions. But we are told that the signature is illegible. The letter is, moreover, inconsistent. This, taken together with the imagery of the snakes, alerts the reader to the likelihood of further deception.

The love scene with Frieda, the barmaid, which follows shortly after K. receives the letter, provides a further clue. As they embrace in "the small puddles of beer" beneath the counter, K. "was haunted by the feeling that he was losing himself or wandering into a strange country, farther than ever man had wandered before, a country so strange that not even the air had anything in common with his native air, where one might die of strangeness, and yet whose enchantment was such that one could only go on and lose oneself further." Their love-making only serves to remind K. of the impossible happiness he was seeking. Frieda's mother describes him as a stranger, a man who isn't wanted and is in everybody's way, who is always causing trouble, a man with obscure intentions. Never forget, she warns him, that "you're the most ignorant person in the village, and be cautious." Ignorant, K. indeed is—ignorant of how impotent the self is against the mechanism of society, of how the social fiction can unman one, stripping him of his freedom and autonomy, ignorant finally of the depths of his own anxiety. He is really too ignorant to be cautious. Thus he pursues his goal by arranging for an interview with the Mayor, a scene that is one of the most revealing in the entire novel. K. is somewhat surprised to discover how easy it was to obtain the appointment. He foolishly assumes that his importance has finally been recognized by officialdom and even more foolishly takes this to be a sign of hope even though he knows from experience that "such fits of easy confidence" are a sign of danger.

K. meets with the Mayor, who is ill with the gout, in a small, unaired room. He again experiences a "sense of extraordinary ease in intercourse with the authorities." But the Mayor comes abruptly to the point with the "plain unvarnished truth of the matter"—which is that the village hasn't the slightest need of a land-surveyor. "The frontiers of our little state are marked out and all officially recorded. So what should we do with a land-surveyor?" The Mayor goes on in a somewhat oily manner to explain how the misunderstanding probably happened. "In such a large governmental office as the Count's, it may occasionally happen that one department ordains this, another that; neither knows of the other, and though the supreme control is absolutely efficient, it comes by its nature too late, and so every now and then a trifling miscalculation arises." The tone is at once pompous and conciliatory, like that of a press secretary. He plays down the mistake by praising the effectiveness of the machine, ignoring the larger matter that K. is dimly aware of: namely, that the whole system may be corrupt and no communication of any kind ever takes place. Kafka emphasizes the irony of this by calling the reader's attention to the great piles of papers and records that fill the room. The Mayor continues with a long-winded, officious explanation of how the mistake arose, which borders on the absurd and yet has an amazing ring of authenticity. At one point he interrupts himself to ask K. if he is bored. No, only amused, K. answers. The Mayor protests that it is not his intention to amuse. Then, in a profound line, K. says: "It only amuses me because it gives me an insight into the ludicrous bungling that in certain circumstances may decide the life of a human being."

The life in question, of course, is K.'s own. He is about to learn that so far he hasn't made any progress whatsoever in his efforts to establish his identity or contact the Castle.

It turns out that he misinterpreted the letter he received. It didn't mean what he thought it did. Furthermore, the phone used on the night of his arrival was not connected. The Mayor tells K. bluntly: "You haven't once up to now come into real contact with our authorities. All those contacts of yours have been illusory, but because of your ignorance of the circumstances you take them to be real. And as for the telephone: in my place, as you see, though I've certainly enough to do with the authorities, there's no telephone . . . There's no fixed connection with the Castle, no central exchange that transmits our calls further." K. is told that some minor official probably monitored his call and played a practical joke on him by saying that he was employed. Bored functionaries do that sort of thing all the time, especially at night. K. begins to understand what he is up against and "that everything is very uncertain and insoluble" in the strange world of the village. K.'s existence is now clearly "threatened by a scandalous official bureaucracy" and he redoubles his efforts. But to no avail. He is no nearer his objective at the end of the novel than he was in the beginning. As Greenberg says, the whole novel is a "marching in place not only in the sense that K. never advances any nearer his goal, but also in the sense that its apparently diverse episodes and occasions and individual histories are only aspects of the story's one matter."* As the novel nears

---

* Greenberg, in *The Terror of Art: Kafka and Modern Literature*, sees K. engaged in the romantic effort to unite concreteness and universality (p. 187). The village is life in all its immediacy while the Castle is abstract thinking about life, a world enslaved to abstract necessity. K. is striving to "unite being and thinking; concrete life and abstract thinking-about-life; spontaneous, self-evident existence and reflective self-awareness seeking justification; unconsciousness and consciousness; sensual heedlessness and stuporousness and spiritual care and clarity; submission to the automatism of the world as a member of the common life, and freedom from the automatism of the world in the solitariness of introspective thinking" (p. 158). Again: "K. seeks being and consciousness, the innocence of

its end the absurdity of K.'s situation is reduced to the comic and pathetic.

I want now to turn to a very different kind of work. John Osborne's *Inadmissible Evidence* cannot compare with *The Castle* as a work of art. But its imagery of alienation makes it very relevant to our discussion here. The play opens in a dreamlike atmosphere of a courtroom, where William Maitland is on trial for his misspent life. His crime is a failure to cope with a mad world that believes in "the technological revolution" and "rapid change." He stands alone conducting his own case, confused and racked by pain. His glands feel like "broken marbles" and his eyelids are like "oysters." He cannot see very clearly and "seems to have lost his drift." He has never had freedom on his side. "I am incapable of making decisions." He is almost forty years old and "never made a decision which I didn't either regret, or suspect was just plain commonplace or shifty or scamped and indulgent or mildly stupid or undistinguished." He took up the practice of law—specializing in divorces—for no particular reason. "The law is to be exploited just like it does us." The scene then fades back to the beginning of a typical day in his office. His assistants and secretary enter. There is light banter (mostly about sex); the mail has to be attended to, the day's work discussed. Maitland emerges as one of the disaffected children of our times, *de trop* in a computerized society. Taxis pass him by; the caretaker turns his back on him, he bears a razor wound as a sign of the pain of existence. Eventually he loses his business and family and disintegrates as a person. He has been unwittingly caught up and defeated

Paradise and the freedom of self which the Tree of Knowledge confers; he wants to have Adam's apple and eat it too. He wants to unite the village and the Castle" (p. 167). On this interpretation, K.'s mission is an impossible struggle to save the world by "transforming its necessity into freedom."

by an endless cycle of consumption and production, of progress and change—of never-ending change. The circle of his life becomes increasingly smaller and he is reduced at last to "catatonic immobility," to total alienation.

The play is punctuated by a series of telephone conversations in which no communication ever takes place. (A situation not unlike that encountered in *The Castle*.) In fact, most of the time we are not even sure there is a connection. The difficulties of mastering a simple switchboard are magnified to symbolize the "ambiguity of reality." This symbolism is convincingly reinforced by the constant reference to divorce cases which depict the brokenness of human life with mute eloquence. Maitland lives in constant fear of being "cut off." He expresses his fears to his wife in swollen, disjointed language: "Sometimes I think you're my only grip left, if you let me go, I'll disappear, I'll be made to disappear, nothing will work, I'll be like something in a capsule in space, weightless, unable to touch anything or do anything, like a groping baby in a removed, putrefying womb . . ." In point of fact, Maitland is cut off. He has expertly diagnosed his own case—except the tense is present rather than future. When he is talking with his daughter toward the end of the play his disintegration becomes more apparent. "There isn't any place for me. In the law, in the country, or, indeed, in any place in this city." He dramatizes his own plight by comparison with his daughter's generation. They don't know passion, guilt or the gnawing worm of self-consciousness. Their "frozen innocence" is what separates them from Maitland. "You'll have done everything well and sensibly and stylishly," he tells her. "You will have to be blown out, snuffed decently, and not be watched spluttering and spilling and hardening." There is, of course, a good deal of ranting and self-pity in Maitland. But that is part of his alienated condition. There is also cruel irony in that he is basically *wrong* about his daughter's generation. But that is because he is wrong about himself as well. He simply does not see clearly. As the curtain falls Maitland is sitting beside a dead phone will his pills, waiting for . . . nothing in particular. He has reached a state of psychic "weightlessness."*

While I do not believe that the play can be considered a great work of social criticism, it is nonetheless impressive by reason of its intense imagery of estrangement. To summarize, there is first of all the constantly evoked presence of the modern city which has been a central symbol of alienation from Wordsworth through Dickens and Baudelaire to any number of present-day writers. *Fourmillante cité,* the ant hill that makes community impossible and divorce necessary. The metropolis is often portrayed as a kind of cancer that feeds on human substance, or a wasteland in which nothing grows, the "unreal city" of Eliot's poems. This cancerous air of unreality pervades Osborne's play. Secondly, the telephone symbolizes the dominion of technology and repressive objectivity. Most directly, the telephone is symbolic of the inability to communicate, but more broadly, it suggests man's dependence on the machine as well as the cold impersonality and lack of freedom that prevails in modern society. The dead phone is the spiritual deadness of the times. This image is reinforced, as I noted, by the divorce motif that runs through the play. Thirdly,

---

* Osborne's play bears comparison with Sartre's *Nausea.* What Erich Kahler says of the Sartre novel is quite applicable to *Inadmissible Evidence:* "It is the story of the gradual decomposition of the substance of our phenomenal world. First of all, decomposition of all abstraction and rational explanation, of all general terms and concepts; and then the decomposition of objects and their qualities, of the images of objects, and of human perception; decomposition of all coherence altogether . . ." Objects dissolve before reason's gaze and finally reason itself dissolves.

there is the theme of man as a stranger to society and to himself. At the end Maitland is alone. He has been abandoned by his family, his staff, his mistress. He lacks, it is true, the romantic grandeur of a Meurseault and other existential strangers. But he is just as pathetic in his lonely desperation. Finally, there are the images of disease. Maitland's alcoholism and headaches, his pills and eventual mental collapse, remind us that the root meaning of alienation is insanity. The prototype of alienated man is the lunatic. "I saw the best minds of my generation destroyed by madness, starving hysterical naked," in Ginsberg's well-known line.

Society and Its Discontents

A lion's share of describing alienated man and his world has fallen to social criticism. As Robert Nisbet points out: "At the present time, in all the social sciences, the various synonyms of alienation have a foremost place in the studies of human relations. Investigations of the 'unattached,' the 'marginal,' the 'obsessive,' the 'normless' and the 'isolated' individual all testify to the central place occupied by the hypothesis of alienation in contemporary social sciences."[3] Another sociologist remarks that "in one form or another the concept of alienation dominates both the contemporary literature and history of sociological thought. It is also a central theme in the classics of Marx, Weber and Durkheim."[4] The assumption underlying social criticism is that self-realization is the result of a satisfying interaction between the self and the world. Alienation, consequently, is viewed as some form of nonparticipation; the individual is not rewardingly connected with any context; his needs (for identity, self-respect, and so forth) are frustrated by the contrary demands of the social structure in which he lives. Such non-participative relationships are well illustrated in the comparison of society to a huge machine. Thus we speak pejoratively of the political machine, of the assembly line, of bureaucratic organization. When we refer popularly to "the system" we are talking about those machine-like organs of society which control vital aspects of our lives independently of what we might think, desire or actually do. In sociological jargon, alienation occurs when person-environment transactions become discordant.

To put it simply, alienated man begins to take on the characteristics of those mechanized agencies which control his life. He becomes reified, thing-like. Marx, the fountainhead of contemporary social criticism, analyzed alienation in precisely these terms. He inherited from Hegel a firm conviction that reality was divided, separated, alienated. But whereas Hegel held that reality was constituted in this way, Marx was not inclined to accept alienation as a permanent, metaphysical feature of "the way things are." Rather he came to consider it a function of society, and of capitalistic society in particular. The problem of alienation was essentially the plight of man under given political and economic conditions. Marx's original insight was to see alienation as the reduction of human substance to the status of a natural object, the transformation of something organic and human into a thing under the capitalistic modes of production. In such economic circumstances the humanistic ideal of men living harmoniously in community, freely developing their natures and satisfying their needs through creative action, could not be realized. "The worker becomes poorer the more wealth he produces, the more his production increases in power and extent," Marx writes. "The worker becomes a cheaper commodity the more commodities he produces. The *increase in value* of the world of things is directly proportional to the *decrease in value* of the human world. Labor not only produces commodities. It also produces itself and the worker as a *commodity* . . ."[5] Thus is the laborer diminished in his work, thingified and made object-like. Given Marx's experiences in the industrial Europe of the nineteenth century, it was altogether natural that he should have formulated the problem of alienation in social terms and considered the worker the prime victim of the economic processes, the very type, as it were, of alienated man in reference to whom all other forms of alienation are to be explained.*

Natural, too, that his criticism should have focused in a special way on the power of money. Money, he said, "abases all the gods of mankind, and changes them into commodities. Money is the universal and self-sufficient value of all things. It has, therefore, deprived the whole world, both the human world and nature, of their proper value. Money is the alienated essence of man's work and existence; this essence dominates him and he worships it."[6] Marx wrote about money with all the fervor of the moralist he remained first

---

* Thus the worker is not only alienated from the product of his labor (and the external, sensuous world at large) but also from his life activity, the act of production. The sources of man's own creative powers are turned against him. Thirdly, just as alienated labor separates man from nature and from himself, so too does it separate him from fellowship with the community of men. When labor is not a free activity but a degrading means to physical existence, man's very humanity is compromised. The vital, organic bonds which should unite the human community give way to a state of detachment in which men appear as non-human objects. Thus in the end man is estranged from his own humanity as well as his fellow-man. Marx had a very keen and demanding sense of community as well as the role of labor in promoting it.

and foremost. He saw it primarily as a *power,* an omnipotent, alien force intruding in man's life. With money one can be what one is not; indeed, we can take on the properties of money itself. What we are, therefore, and can do, is not determined by our humanity but by our purchasing power. If we are ugly, we can buy beauty; if we are dishonorable, money can make us honorable; we may be stupid "but since money is the *real mind* of all things, how should its possessor be stupid?" Thus does money, magic-like, transform all things into their opposites. It is a "disruptive power for the individual and for the social bonds. It changes fidelity into infidelity, love into hate, hate into love, virtue into vice, vice into virtue, servant into master, stupidity into intelligence and intelligence into stupidity." It confuses and transposes the natural order of things; it is the "universal agent of separation." It is alienating because it is merely an external means of power; it transforms the human and natural into abstractions and conversely transforms mere fancies into "real faculties and powers." In the human world, Marx writes, there are values that cannot be bought. Love can only be exchanged for love, trust for trust, and so on. The human order is only falsified and contradicted by money's almost divine powers of conversion.

Marx's hatred of money has the marked melodramatic flavor that is found in much Victorian fiction; it is at once grotesque, utopian and moralistic. But it also contains an important kernel of truth. By denouncing the worship of Mammon he joined a venerable tradition which attributed self-alienation to acquisition. This had long been an abiding theme of the Christian moralists, for example, and increasingly a theme in literature since the Renaissance. Marx himself quotes at some length Shakespeare's *Timon of Athens* where money is referred to as "the common whore of mankind" and the "bright defiler of Hymen's purest bed." From this point of view he can be compared with those who saw a parallel between the alienative power of money and the abstractions of scientific method and rationalist metaphysics. These abstractions have been roundly denounced as agents of appropriation, instruments of distancing man from himself and his society. When the exchange value of commodities replaces their use value, a purely quantitative world comes between man and man. Concrete human relationships are replaced by a purely commercial relationship of sellers and buyers. Modern man has become so depersonalized, Lewis Mumford writes ominously, that he can no longer stand up to his machines. When the qualitative dimension of life is eliminated from the human world, the worker (and today this includes nearly everyone) becomes an interchangeable element in a rational calculus, measuring out his days by installment payments and tax returns. Human relationships take on the tinny, brittle character of the profit motive, and one's psychic life becomes an extension of things. Quite simply, one's worth is measured by an economic standard. This forces man to become more and more like an automaton, passively submitting to social laws that are totally foreign to his real needs. The quest for subjective authenticity, for ethical wholeness, is limited to a strict minority in such a society.

Social thinkers since Marx's time have continued to explore the problem of alienation and society. It is a major perspective in nineteenth- as well as twentieth-century social commentary. One thinks of such an influential work as Ferdinand Tönnies' *Gemeinschaft and Gesellschaft,* first published in 1887. The distinction in the title points to two quite different kinds of human associations. *Gemeinschaft* signifies an organic relationship, a community, exemplified primarily in the family. *Gesellschaft,* on the other hand, indicates separation, tension and dislocation. Tönnies argues that modern history has evolved progressively toward *Gesellschaft.* He cites the rise of science (with its handmaiden, technology) and the Industrial Revolution as the principal contributory forces to this trend. Community allows the expression of man's integral nature—his drives, desires and dispositions. Society, under the dominion of science and industry, is governed by narrow cognitive processes and allows only fragmentary expression of man's nature. Man's cognitive functions have become isolated from his whole being. Max Weber's analysis of society was in a similar vein. He had no faith that socialism would be any better than capitalism. Both were expressions of a more fundamental force which he called "rationalization." By this he meant the conversion of traditional social values into the bureaucratic forms of modern life. He foresaw and dreaded the coming of technological man. In a passage that might have been written by a Kafka, he writes: "It is horrible to think that the world could one day be filled with nothing but those little cogs, little men clinging to little jobs and striving towards the bigger ones. This passion for bureaucracy is enough to drive one to despair. It is as if in politics . . . we were deliberately to become men who need 'order' and nothing but order, become nervous and cowardly if for one moment this order wavers, and helpless if they are torn away from their total incorporation in it. That the world should know no men but these: it is in such an evolution that we are already caught up, and the great question is, therefore, not how we can promote and hasten it, but what can we oppose to this machinery in order to keep a portion of mankind free from this parceling-out of the soul, from this supreme mastery of the bureaucratic way of life." Weber predicted

that Western man was entering a "polar night of icy darkness and hardness" and he wonders hauntingly who of us
will be alive when the long night recedes and what will have
become of us. "Will you be bitter or banausic?" Weber asks.

Karl Mannheim thought the intellectuals would be able
to solve the social problem. He reasoned that if our thinking
is determined by our social status, if each segment of society
has a different point of view which in the long run proves
divisive, then the universal truth that could unify such conflicting views would have to be provided precisely by a
universal socially unattached class whose grasp of reality
was comprehensive. His hope, expressed in *Ideology and
Utopia*, now seems a vain one. In the society of today there
is no universal class. The works of artists and intellectuals
have themselves become commodities—subject to the iron
laws of the marketplace. Georg Simmel also set himself
against the "rationalist individualism" of his society. The
eighteenth-century promise of human fulfillment and liberation had not been made good; man in the modern metropolis
is not a whole creature. His social self is lost among the over-
powering objective forces of industrial society while his
private self retreats to the solipsistic depths of subjectivity.
Simmel spoke of alienation as the "collision between society
and the individual" and he is in the mainstream of post-
Marxian social criticism when he writes that "the individual
has become a mere cog in an enormous organization of
things and powers which tear from his hands all progress,
spirituality, and value in order to transform them from their
subjective form into the form of a purely objective life."
His comments on the psychic hazards of city life are incisive.
The metropolis is the arena of a culture that is inimical to
personal life. "Here in buildings and educational institutions,
in the wonders and comforts of space-conquering technol-

ogy, in the formations of community life, and in the visible institutions of the state, is offered such an overwhelming fullness of crystallized and impersonalized spirit that the personality, so to speak, cannot maintain itself under its impact."

Another penetrating nineteenth-century analysis of social alienation can be found in the works of Emile Durkheim. He noted that such states as boredom and anxiety cannot as a rule be found in pre-modern societies. Yet there is a high incidence of them in a complex society like our own. Durkheim developed the concept of "anomie" to describe a social condition in which there are no commonly accepted rules to guide conduct. He first advanced this concept in a study on the division of labor. In a highly differentiated society with its concomitant specialization the "collective conscience" tends to weaken and anonymity increases. The concept was applied more forcefully in another, later study on suicide, which Durkheim found increased in periods of economic depression and prosperity. The reason was the same in both cases: a sudden disruption of the economic scale making goals unattainable. In times of depression people lack the economic wherewithal to satisfy their needs and suffer from a lowering in their social status. In times of prosperity, on the other hand, a kind of "the sky is the limit" mood sets in and aspirations tend to soar to the limitless. Confusion is the result, and perspectives becomes distorted. In both times of depression and prosperity there is a breakdown in the normative structure of society. Durkheim believed that the modern age is one of great prosperity and limitless striving. It is necessarily an age of great anxiety and alienation as well. This is the absurd price of progress. "What could be more disillusioning," he writes, "than to proceed toward a terminal point that is nonexistent, since it recedes in the same measure that one advances? . . . This is why historical periods like ours, which have known the malady of infinite aspiration, are necessarily touched with pessimism. Pessimism always accompanies unlimited aspirations. Goethe's *Faust* may be regarded as representing par excellence this view of the infinite. And it is not without reason that the poet has portrayed him as laboring in continual anguish."

These questions continue to be widely discussed in the current literature of social criticism. Our problems today are, of course, much more complex and all social situations are profoundly more ambiguous. The quest for a society in which the conditions for human realization will be maximized goes on at a frantic pace; we seek the human reality that must subtend all social realities. It is a good time for prophets of a new order. But the quest is an increasingly difficult one; we appear to be helpless to remedy our situation. A great war machine with the power to annihilate all human life on this planet many times over now most conspicuously clouds the horizon of our hopes and efforts. This is the new, numbing reality that earlier social critics did not have to deal with, nor could they have anticipated it, and subordinates all of our problems to a literal problem of survival. The overkill bomb has now become the central symbol of the fact that there has never been a time when we felt more excluded from the fateful decisions affecting our lives (and deaths). It is as though we were matching our wits against some superior intelligence that is bent on our destruction. One has to run hard just to remain in the same place, a predicament reminiscent of the medieval legend of the Wild Hunt in which the souls of the dead had to march night and day at great speed. There was no goal in view, and when anyone fell from exhaustion, he immediately crumbled into dust. We can read in this a parable of alienated man who is threatened with extinction by an increasingly nihilistic social order.

The Imprisoning Self

This awareness is no doubt one reason why much alienation talk today is in psychological terms, with the emphasis on the problems of self rather than those of society. In the final analysis, of course, the two dimensions cannot be separated. There is a necessary interaction between self and society such that when the balance is upset on either side some form of alienation sets in. Thus, the conditions of society can create problems for the self. Conversely, sick people are likely to create a sick society. There is an inherent circularity here that makes it very dangerous to talk of alienation as anything other than a disrupted relationship between the two. Alienation from society and alienation from self are the two limiting points of a same continuum. Consider, for example, anxiety, which is one of the principal psychological cognates for alienation. The word derives from the Latin *angustia* and literally means a shortness of breath, with overtones of cramped, unaired living quarters. "My emotions need space," wrote Rilke in protest against the confinement of modern life. This sense of anxiety as oppressive constriction is well symbolized in German mythology by the Midgard serpent: a great beast which encircles and holds our world in its grip. All of our experiences are thus limited and confined by its monstrous coils. Each time the great beast moves a muscle our identities are threatened and we are filled with nameless fears. We might compare the serpent to society and conclude that the self has no hope of fulfillment. But we might also compare it to the self and conclude that some original sin has infected it, making it inherently defective and therefore prone to produce alien worlds. The Midgard myth is not decisive either way; it illustrates the effects of anxiety more than the cause of it.

Freud's analysis of human nature also allows for either interpretation. He considered the universe to be basically hostile to man, and held (in *The Future of an Illusion*, for example) that the principal task of civilization is to defend him against nature. On the other hand, the self is dominated by an inherited death instinct whose aim is to reduce the living organism to an inorganic state. The self is divided between the epic struggle of Eros and Thanatos and there is never any doubt about the outcome. Likewise with the conflict between the id and the superego, between the innate, pleasure-seeking drive of the self and socially imposed coercion and repression. When Freud formulated the problem of alienation as the insoluble conflict between the pleasure and reality principles, he was saying in so many words that it derives from both self and society which have been juxtaposed to one another by an inexorable fate. What is imposed by society is internalized by the self so that the tension between freedom and repression, love and destruction, the instinctual and the intellectual becomes the inner principle of civilization and has led in our time to a completely alienated world. Herbert Marcuse sees Freud's theory of alienation manifested in the ironic contrast between modern man's scientific sophistication and his psychic impoverishment. The human agency which succeeded so well in transforming the natural environment revealed itself as an essentially offensive and aggressive subject set over against an object. Along with Binswanger, Scheler and many other thinkers, Marcuse attributes this subject-object dichotomy (which lies at the root of all forms of alienation) to the rise of analytic logic, that is to say, the reduction of the laws of thought to techniques of calculation and manipulation. "Since the canonization of Aristotelian logic, Logos merges with the idea of ordering, classifying, mastering reason. And this idea of reason becomes increasingly antagonistic to those faculties and attitudes which are receptive rather than productive, which tend toward gratification rather than transcendence, which remain strongly committed to the pleasure principle. The Logos shows forth as the logic of domination. When logic then reduces the units of thought to signs and symbols, the laws of thought have finally become techniques of calculation and manipulation. The Logos of gratification contradicts the Logos of alienation: the effort to harmonize the two animates the inner history of Western metaphysics."[7] Marcuse sees a straight line from Aristotle to Hegel, who made the last great effort to both justify and cancel out the fact of alienation. This is an important insight.* It is a way of thinking that seems clearly to attribute the main source of alienation to man himself, and sees it as an outcome of his anxieties, his need for self-idealization, his misuse of his creative potential. Karen Horney was prominent among those who saw alienation as an inevitable result of neurotic

---

* I would, however, want to qualify it. In Greek metaphysics logic was not, as a matter of fact, an instrument of alienation; it was rather an organ of intelligibility, a means of seeing the world more clearly and getting the self and society into more satisfactory rapport. But Marcuse is right insofar as Greek metaphysics and logic were later put to work powerfully toward alienation. It was not, I think, until the triumph of Augustinian Christianity—with its negation of life instincts, institutionalized guilt and delayed hope—that the shape of alienation as we know it today emerged. It was only after the world became the enemy that logic could be used as an instrument of exploitation. I shall have more to say on this in Part II.

development. Alienation is "the remoteness of the neurotic from his own feelings, wishes, beliefs and energies. It is the loss of the feeling of being an active determining force in his own life. It is the loss of feeling himself an organic whole. These in turn indicate an alienation from the most alive center of ourselves which I have suggested calling the real self."[8]

There are admittedly great difficulties with a term like "real self." Contemporary philosophers are, on the whole, inclined to shy away from it because it smacks too much of old-school metaphysics. But Horney found the concept useful for therapeutic purposes. For her the real self referred to the constructive forces in the individual that must be identified and developed. Thus she spoke of the real self as providing what William James called the "inward palpitating life." It engenders a "spontaneity of feelings." It is the source of "spontaneous interests and energies." It is also "the capacity to wish and to will, the part of ourselves which wishes to grow and expand and fulfill itself." This real self, when strong and active, enables us to make decisions and assume responsibility for them. It leads to "genuine integration and a sound sense of wholeness, oneness. Not merely are body and mind, need and thought or feeling, consonant and harmonious, but they function without serious inner conflict."

In this sense, then, alienation occurs when the constructive forces of the real self are blocked, when the individual is distanced from the sources of his growth. A clinical profile of an alienated person would show one who suffered from or was prone to depersonalization, amnesia, hysteria, schizophrenia and depression. He would likely show such symptoms as lack of body expressions (eyes, face, etc.), unresponsiveness to things and persons, hazy thinking, an inability to grasp the implication of situations, memory blackouts, indifference and superficiality with respect to his past, family, possessions and even life itself and an insensitivity toward others. The key words here are mechanical, passive, detached. Such a condition is characterized by a sensation of living in a fog, with little or no emotional reaction to events, little or no sense of at-homeness or of life as a continuous enterprise. In *The Divided Self* Ronald Laing gives us a vivid description of an alienated person in his analysis of Julie, a twenty-six-year-old chronic schizophrenic. She had been a patient in a mental ward for nine years and had become typically "inaccessible and withdrawn." She was "hallucinated, given to posturing, to stereotyped, bizarre, incomprehensible actions . . . In clinical psychiatric terminology, she suffered from depersonalization, derealization, autism, nihilistic delusions, delusions of persecution, omnipotence; she had ideas of reference and end-of-the-world phantasies, auditory hallucinations, impoverishment of affects, etc." When she spoke with her doctors, Julie said she could not find happiness. She felt unreal as though there were "an invisible barrier between herself and others." She spoke of being "crushed," "smothered," "burned up" by hostile forces that never left her alone. She was aware of being alone, emptied and destructive. Her self-understanding was entirely in the images of alienation. She was "born under a black sun," she compared herself to "a ruined city," "a broken picture," "a well run dry." She is, in a word, existentially dead or, as in Laing's terminology, an "unembodied self." Consequently she is prevented from directly participating in experience. The unembodied self participates in nothing directly; rather it engages almost entirely in second-order activities.

From the psychological point of view, we may say in sum

that alienation is synonymous with an incoherent sense of self, with psychic disorganization. Dealienation depends upon the conviction that one's endeavors and life make sense, that they are constantly replenished at the well-springs of meaning, that the varying facets of experience are integral units of a grasped whole. Even from the strictest psychological view, self-alienation is rarely an isolated phenomenon; it always goes together with alienation from others and the world around us. The self is not an abstract entity, something we look for—like a needle in a haystack. It is something realized through appropriate action. That is why to speak of "the search for identity" is misleading when not in fact false. Identity is not searched out, as though it were already there but only hidden. Horney herself was quick to point out that alienation is largely a problem of the individual's stance toward social norms and culturally conditioned patterns of behavior. Thus the terminology of alienation again directs our attention to man's being-in-the-world and asserts that alienation is always some defect in the experiencing process, some form of divorce between self and world.

Psychology, however, is not always able to respect the integrity of this process. As existentially inclined psychologists like Erwin Straus point out, because psychology is indebted to scientific method for many of its procedural techniques, it must often abstract from the world in its "sensory splendor." This creates a basic difficulty: "When experience is quantified in this way it must at the same time be debased epistemologically and metaphysically devaluated." Straus views the scientific manipulation of sensory experience as a basic misconception of experiencing as such, "the mode of being of experiencing creatures." He further links this dichotomy to the unfavorable interpretations of the senses and emotions that have predominated in the development of modern philosophy. Straus quite rightly sees that our problems with alienation today have their origins in philosophical assumptions, particularly the assumption "that consciousness with all its numerous contents is alone with itself, cut off from the world."[9] Modern times begin, J. H. Miller concurs, when man confronts his isolation, his separation from everything outside of himself. He goes on to point out that the presupposition of the isolated self stems from Montaigne, Descartes and Locke in the seventeenth century and forms an unbroken tradition down to present-day existentialism.[10]

The Fallacy of Isolation

Although the concept of alienation is a multi-faceted one, with various definitions and descriptions, the idea of the isolated self brings us close to the heart of what it means. We can best understand it as one form or another of what Professor Heinemann has called "the fallacy of isolation"— principally the isolation of consciousness from the external world and the assumption that discursive reasoning and life are antithetical. Heinemann's definition of alienation seems to me a good one: "The facts to which the term alienation refers are, objectively, different kinds of disassociation, break or rupture between human beings and their objects, whether the latter be other persons, or the natural world, or their own creations of art, science and society; and, subjectively, the corresponding states of disequilibrium, disturbance, strangeness and anxiety."[11] I have already spoken of "disconnection" as a synonym for alienation. We might also speak of "separation" in this context. An alienated world is one in which the parts are indeed separated out, a world that exhibits intractable forms of fragmentation and irreducible polarities. This is a common feature of whatever form of alienation we might encounter; it is always some determination of disunion or separateness. But what must be further noted is that what essentially defines alienation is not separation as such— for some kinds of separation are desirable—but the Humpty Dumpty plight of not being able to put the separated parts together in any scheme of meaningful relationships. An alienated world is thus more precisely one in which reality is seen to be fundamentally contradictory in nature and impervious to the unifying efforts of thought and valuation.

Existentialist philosophy, no doubt the principal expression of our contemporary awareness of alienation,* stresses this contradictory aspect of reality under the rubric of absurdity. Absurdity is the experience of those who discover an unbridgeable gulf between reason and experience,

---

* I think it worth mentioning here that the more analytic schools of philosophy also reflect modern man's concern with alienation. Professor Mora, for example, considers Wittgenstein as a "symbol of troubled times." His argument is that analytic philosophy is fragmentary and piecemeal and as such indicative of the fragmentation prevalent in society. The ultimate tendency of Wittgenstein's thought, says Mora, was the suppression of all thought. Thinking is the greatest perturbing factor of human life, a sign of sickness. No language is adequate to the expression of ideas. "Wittgenstein was one of the gloomiest spokesmen of our times," Mora observes. "He did describe our 'age of anxiety' and our 'age of longing' better than anybody else—better than poets, better than novelists." (See J. F. Mora, "Wittgenstein: A Symbol of Troubled Times," *Philosophy and Phenomenological Research,* Vol. XV (1953), pp. 89 ff. The strong emphasis of analytic philosophy on formal consistency is, Louis Kampf has pointed out, no more than the reverse side of chaos. "If we take the imposed relationships of a closed system to be the only measure of order, then, who knows, the world as a whole might indeed be totally disordered; and to complete the vicious circle, if there is nothing but chaos, any arbitrary order we impose will do." See his *On Modernism* (Cambridge, M.I.T. Press, 1967), p. 318.

between the self and what is not the self. Thus, in *The Myth of Sisyphus* Camus speaks of the absurd as a confrontation of "a non-rational world by that desperate desire for clarity which is one of man's needs." Again: "The divorce between man and his life, the actor and his setting, is properly the feeling of absurdity." The mind and the world "strain at each other without being able to embrace each other." This sense of alienation arises in different ways. Perhaps it is the mechanical nature of our lives, the deadening routine of bureaucratic life, that first leads us to raise the question of life's meaning. "It happens that the stage sets collapse. Rising, street-car, four hours in the office or the factory, meal, street-car, four hours of work, meal, sleep and Monday Tuesday Wednesday Thursday Friday and Saturday according to the same rhythm—this path is easily followed most of the time. But one day the 'why' arises and everything begins in that weariness tinged with amazement." When the stage of our action is suddenly deprived through lucid inquiry of its conventional props, then man "feels an alien, a stranger." Or it may be our sense of time's passing and the inevitability of death that makes life appear absurd. Too, it may be the dense contingency of a physical world that is alien to us that gives rise to awareness of absurdity. "The word is dense, at the heart of all beauty lies something inhuman." It is perhaps most often our intercourse with others that provokes the unhappy thought that we are irremediably alone, others who don't respond to our needs for intimacy and communion, who treat us like things. These are all so many ways in which the self comes to unsatisfactory terms with experience.

Most existential writing on alienation has a harsh, transempirical tone with an almost religious stress on the inevitability as well as the hopelessness of this condition. Paul

Tillich is a case in point. He writes unequivocally: "The state of our whole life is estrangement from others and from ourselves because we are estranged from the ground of our being, because we are estranged from the origin and aim of our life. We do not know where we have come from or where we are going." There are Gnostic overtones in a statement like this that imply a radical dualism with respect to all realms of being—God and world, spirit and matter, good and evil, etc. The world is an alienated shadow of some aboriginal harmony and unity. To be born is to take leave of a pure realm and fall to an inferior level of estranged existence. From a Gnostic viewpoint alienation neither originates with man nor can it be remedied by him. Tillich, not surprisingly, is critical of those who say that it is a human phenomenon and therefore capable of being overcome by human means. He has in mind Marx and psychologists like Jung and Fromm who, he claims, have abandoned Freud's insight concerning the depth of human estrangement. This, says Tillich, is to take too superficial a view of the matter. Although he has respect for the many analyses of man in industrial society which underscore self-loss and world-loss, emptiness and meaninglessness, he considers them basically fallacious insofar as they hold that alienation derives from the structure of a particular society or can be attributed to specific circumstances. On the other hand, neither does Tillich agree with those who say that there is no possibility of overcoming alienation. His religious interests and his method of correlation (i.e. biblical answers to existential problems) commit him to a salvation philosophy. What man de facto is can be learned from existential analyses; what he is ideally can be learned from biblical revelation, from a supra-human source. Human nature is fundamentally but not ultimately estranged. Tillich's solution to the prob-

lem of alienation has the strength and weaknesses of all
fideist positions. His extensive reworking of traditional
religious and metaphysical language (God-above-God,
ultimate concern, non-being, etc.) does not finally conceal
the fact that his solution is a very traditional one: resort
to a mystical a priori, to an immediate intuition of something ultimate which transcends all mundane distinctions
and strivings. Revelation, of one sort or another, is the only
answer to the human predicament. This is a typically
Gnostic stance.

The Gnostic strain is less pronounced in a writer like
Sartre. That is to say, he rejects solutions of supernatural
provenance although he predicates a radical alienation of
the human condition. As the atheistic heir of Descartes and
Hegel, Sartre is haunted by the specter of the isolated self,
that nebulous offspring of an unhappy marriage between
essence and existence. He begins with the assumption that
man is a divided, alien, anguished being. As Iris Murdoch
remarks, the human person is for Sartre supported by
"neither the steady pattern of divine purpose, nor the reliable constellation of Newtonian physics, nor the dialectical
surge of work and struggle. His universe is solipsistic. Other
people enter it, one at a time, as the petrifying gaze of the
Medusa, or at best as the imperfectly understood adversary
in the fruitless conflict of love. What determines the form of
this egocentric and non-social world are the movements of
love and hate, project and withdrawal, embarrassment and
domination, brooding and violence . . ."[12] In *Being and
Nothingness* Sartre offers two incommensurate modes of
being (being-in-itself and being-for-itself) as his basic philosophical postulates. They support his world like the pillars
of Hercules; they provide the framework of all his later
speculations about man and bar in advance any way out of

the prison of life. The knowing mind is forever colliding with the contextual world. Being-in-itself corresponds roughly to the being of the external world, the world of material things. This world is wholly given, massive, opaque, meaningless. There is no reason for its being. It is simply there, what it is, "superfluous for all eternity." Being-for-itself coincides with the world of human freedom whose nature is to be fluid, incomplete, other than what it is. Being-in-itself is impenetrable, ungraspable, alien. Being-for-itself has no such solidity or identity. It has no fixed place since its nature is always to be one step ahead of itself. The self is that whose essence is not what it is and is what it is not.

The sheer spontaneity of consciousness, that limpid world where anything goes and nothing is justified, gives rise to the experience of forlornness in which the isolated self apprehends the empty reaches of responsibility and gazes enviously upon the solidity of things about it, a world in which structure has collapsed. Antoine Roquentin, that extraordinary protagonist of *Nausea,* is suddenly overcome with an overwhelming sense of his own unreality; his self-awareness flicks on and off like a firefly, growing increasingly more vague and evanescent. Roquentin experiences the full blow of Cartesian doubt and, like Descartes, finds a measure of solace in the pure, clear world of mathematical certainty. Unlike Kafka's K., who cannot analyze the absurdity his actions reflect, Roquentin is reflective, *un homme qui pense.* For Sartre, man is that being whose past is dissolved in the lucid apprehension of the moment which in turn is lost in a hurtling project toward the future, that being whose lack of being renders his choices and values utterly contingent and without connection in the manifold of reality, a creature whose impossible striving toward coincidence with concrete existence is the basis of his alienated predicament. We expand ourselves in a vain effort to reach completeness and totality and in trying to accomplish this goal we are exposed to all the vultures of constant striving. As Sartre put it, following Hegel, human reality is by nature an unhappy consciousness, without the possibility of surpassing its unhappy state.

Yet in addition to the rationalist Sartre, submerged in the nihilism and epistemological ambiguity of the Western philosophical tradition, there is also Sartre the disciple of Marx, Sartre the politician and revolutionary. Since World War II he has been engaged in political affairs (both through his bi-monthly journal, *Les Temps Modernes,* and active participation) and in recent years he has turned more and more to an analysis of man in *society.* This Sartre is much more sensitive to what man is in his historical and economic conditions, to the possibilities of contextual freedom and the interrelationships between men. Thus he dwells on such problems as how the family mediates between the class and the individual; the nature of work and purposeful activity; the overcoming of reification in the specificity of social processes; collectivism and freedom; and so forth. In so doing he has been able to appreciably round out his earlier theories of freedom, responsibility and the nature of reality. The later Sartre is willing to say, for example, that man is in some sense determined by his social conditions. Still, he remains partial to his initial positions and ways of seeing things. The old metaphysical dog does not easily learn new Marxist tricks! Howard Parsons says it well: "In an idealistic tradition dating from Descartes, Sartre assumes the priority of the individual ego, which then generates the world of others. This is a great mistake. From it follow all of Sartre's other mistakes, including the supposition that we can get to socialism by thinking and willing to do so . . . Sartre's view that all human relations are essentially egocentric and exploitive is a perversion . . . If one begins with a world primordialy divided into subject and object, all endeavors to close the division are doomed to inconclusiveness. One cannot begin with individualistic premises and reach socialist conclusions. The conquest of ambiguity will elude Sartre (and all of us) so long as man is in fact alienated from others and the world."[13]

I would argue, in other words, that the principal weakness of the existentialist account of alienation is the circular manner in which its starting point precludes any viable solution. To postulate a radically fissured universe in which unbridgeable splits contend endlessly with one another is to say the least a rather peculiar exercise of rationality. There is no reason why we must accept dualistic assumptions about the kind of world we live in; nor is there any reason why we should agree with the fideist wing of existentialism (Kierkegaard, Buber, Berdyaev, Marcel, etc.) which concludes its assessment of man on a note of mysticism and prescribes various leaps of faith and revelations as a solution to the problem of alienation. This would be tantamount to admitting that the case is *ab initio* hopeless. There is no doubt a sense in which the world is absurd. The existentialists and the vast corpus of alienation literature has made a strong case for as much. But to admit that absurdity is its final status would doom creative reflection to impotence and brutally cancel out mankind's fond hopes that the ugly world's face will one day be transformed into a thing of beauty. The supposition that nature and man are alien to one another in some absolute sense is, as Sterling Lamprecht has pointed out, purely "fantastic."[14]

But this much is now clear: it is in terms of "reality as contradictory" that the problem of alienation can best be approached, formulated and clarified. At the level of language, it most frequently finds expression in such hyphen-ated formulae as thought-being, existence-essence, subject-object, nature-supernature, self-world, being-appearance, mind-body, individual-social, ends-means, and the like. As methodological distinctions and linguistic shortcuts such hyphenations are legitimate and it would be presumptuous to want to do away with them. They do, after all, serve the purposes of analysis with fair adequacy. But when they solidify into rigorous dualisms or split off into isolate "isms" of whatever kind, they fail as instruments of conceptual unity and point to the broken world of alienation. That such dichotomies have often proven difficult, when not impos-sible, to mediate in our cultural history is some indication that alienation has had a long career.

Two questions now quite naturally occur. First, how can alienation be overcome? And, secondly, what ante-cedent cultural factors have made it possible for twentieth-century man to assign central importance to alienation? What historical processes and forces subtend our contem-porary affliction? The first question is perhaps more urgent, but the second has a fundamental priority, for it turns our attention back to the ideological basis of alienation. I should like to stress that one of the best ways of understanding the problem of alienation is to view it in light of certain cultural determinants that are not always sufficiently under-stood. Today, it may safely be granted, the pervasive serious-ness of the problem is most crucially experienced as certain desirable operations to be performed and our felt and proven inability to perform them (i.e. put the fragments back together or mediate the contradictions). Implicit in this experience is an unsatisfactory understanding of how our present predicament came to pass.

□ THE AGE OF ALIENATION

1. Harold Rosenberg, Review of *Alienation: The Cultural Climate of Our Time,* edited by Gerald Sykes, in *New York Times Book Review,* December 20, 1964, p. 1. Sykes' book is a good illustration of how comprehensive the concept of alienation is. One way of reducing this generality is to bear in mind some such schema as the following, suggested by the editors of the *Dictionary of Social Sciences:*
   A. Alienation denotes an estrangement or separation between parts or the whole of personality and significant aspects of the world of experience.
      1. Within this general denotation the term may refer to:
         (a) an objective state of estrangement or separation
         (b) the state of feeling of the estranged personality
         (c) a motivational state tending towards estrangement
      2. The separation denoted by the term may be:
         (a) between the self and the objective world
         (b) between the self and aspects of the self that have become separated and placed over against the self such as alienated labor
         (c) between the self and the self
   B. Although there are several sources for the idea of alienation, its primary source in the social sciences was Marx, supported perhaps by the psychology of Freud.
   C. From this conception of alienation as an objective state of separation, there comes the usage of alienation as the malaise that results from such a state, sometimes accompanied by a shift in emphasis from structures of domination to the value content of the culture as the primary casual factor. This might be called psychological alienation.
   D. Efforts to overcome alienation.

2. Martin Greenberg, *The Terror of Art: Kafka and Modern Literature* (New York, Basic Books, 1965), p. 161.

3. Robert Nisbet, *The Quest for Community* (New York, Oxford, 1953), p. 15. Also valuable for an overview of sociological theory on alienation is Professor Nisbet's *The Sociological Tradition* (New York, Basic Books, 1966) and *The New Sociology: Essays in Social Science and Social Theory in Honor of C. Wright Mills,* edited by Irving Louis Horowitz (New York, Oxford, 1965).

4. Melvin Seeman, "On the Meaning of Alienation," *American Sociological Review,* Vol. XXIV (1959), p. 783. Seeman pre-

sents an organized view of the sociological meanings of alienation by distinguishing five senses in which the world is used:
powerlessness, meaninglessness, normlessness, isolation and
self-estrangement. His classification has been widely commented
upon by sociologists and his terminology is still in currency,
although needless to say there is a good deal of overlapping of
these five different senses.

5. *Writings of the Young Marx*, edited by Loyd D. Easton and
   Kurt H. Guddat (New York, Doubleday, 1967), p. 289.
6. Karl Marx, "Money," in Erich Fromm's *Marx's Concept of
   Man* (New York, Ungar, 1961), pp. 163 ff.
7. Herbert Marcuse, *Eros and Civilization* (New York, Vintage,
   1962), p. 101.
8. Karen Horney, *Neurosis and Human Growth: The Struggle
   Toward Self-Realization* (New York, Norton, 1950), p. 157.
9. Erwin Straus, "Anesthesiology and Hallucinations," in *Existence:
   A New Dimension in Psychiatry and Psychology*, edited by Rollo
   May, Ernest Angel and Henri F. Ellenberger (New York,
   Basic Books, 1958). Some good material on the psychological
   view of alienation can also be found in the *In Memoriam* issue
   to Karen Horney of *The American Journal of Psychoanalysis*,
   Vol. XIV (1964) and *Identity and Anxiety*, edited by Maurice
   Stein, Arthur Vidich and David Manning White (New York,
   The Free Press, 1963).
10. See J. H. Miller, *The Disappearance of God* (Cambridge, Har-
    vard University Press, 1963). Miller takes modern man's situa-
    tion to be "essentially one of disconnection between man and
    nature, between man and man, and even between man and him-
    self" (p. 2). His book is primarily an analysis of the emergence
    of the alienation theme in nineteenth-century British writers. The
    alienation of the writer and artist, Miller believes, reflects the
    initial assumptions of modern philosophy as well as present social
    conditions. The artist goes into the empty spaces left by the lack
    of order and the disappearance of values and "takes the enor-
    mous risk of attempting to create in that vacancy a new fabric
    of connection between man and the divine power" (pp. 13–14).
11. F. H. Heinemann, *Existentialism and the Modern Predicament*
    (New York, Harper Torchbooks, 1953), p. 1. William Levi also
    offers a good descriptive definition of alienation when he writes
    that "in every case the use of the term implies an axiological
    dualism, a valuational contrariety, and the essential pairs in this

case are therefore, I think, three: (1) the unified or integrated versus the divided or fragmented; (2) the organic, the sensed, the human, versus the mechanical, the abstract, the thing-like; and (3) the immediate and feelingful versus the impersonal and distant. *Fragmentation, mechanization, distantiation* are the three dimensions of alienation, and every usage, however remote, will in some sense suppose, or explicate, or explore one or more of these crucial aspects. See his "Existentialism and the Alienation of Man," in *Phenomenology and Existentialism*, edited by Edward N. Lee and Maurice Mandelbaum (Baltimore, The John Hopkins Press, 1967), p. 254.

12. Iris Murdoch, *Sartre: Romantic Rationalist* (New Haven, Yale University Press, 1953), p. 72.

13. Howard Parsons, "Existentialism and Marxism in Dialogue," in *Marxism and Alienation*, edited by Herbert Aptheker (New York, Humanities Press, 1965), pp. 113 ff. Parsons seems to be in agreement with what I have already noted about the self: "The truth is that the self is not a discrete, autonomous thing prior to social relations but emerges within social processes. Social psychology and interpersonal psychiatry make this evident. I am *with* the Other, in dialectical relation to him. I do not understand him by first understanding myself; instead, I discover him, just as I discover myself, as an objective participant in an objective social process" (p. 113).

14. See Sterling Lamprecht, "Naturalism and Religion," in *Naturalism and Human Spirit,* edited by Yervant H. Krokorian (New York, Columbia University Press, 1964). Lamprecht writes: "The world may be alien to some purposes and congenial to others but to speak of the world as alien in some absolute sense is nonsense. The world is alien only to a point of view or an ambition or an interest; and surely the instruction of experience is that men ought to learn to take, then, some other point of view, to adopt some other ambition, to cherish some other interest. To hold rigorously to what is not possible in the kind of world in which we occur and our acts must therefore be performed is a mark, not of exalted morality that is "too good" for the natural realm, but of immature folly that has not yet discovered what morality really is" (p. 29).

Part II

THE

ADVENT OF

ALIENATION

It has become a commonplace to trace the history of alienation from nineteenth-century sources—Hegel and Marx in particular.* On the other hand, many thinkers endeavor to situate its origin much earlier. Some hold that the Christian doctrine of sin (or, more broadly, the Christian ethos as such) is an early paradigm for our modern doctrines of alienation. Others say that the Old Testament teaching on idolatry constitutes the earliest expression of alienation. Still others attribute the source of alienation to Plato's view that the sense world is but a faint picture of the perfect world of ideas. Finally, the Greek salvation philosophies (Stoicism, Skepticism, Epicureanism and what eventually came to be called Neoplatonism) are considered a prime source. There is no doubt some truth in all of these claims. Indeed, as Erich Kahler observes, there is a sense in which the whole history of man could be written as a history of alienation.[1]

But it doesn't help much to say that man has always been alienated. In a very real sense it bypasses the whole problem by making analysis irrelevant. Even if the universalist claim were the case, it would still remain true that there is something distinct about our experience of alienation today. It speaks to a unique dimension in the cultural crisis of our times. My own investigation into the problem leads me to believe that we can detect the distinctive flavor of our modern experience of alienation in the late Middle Ages and Renaissance era—a time that was in the profound-

* See my disagreement with Irving Louis Horowitz on this point in *Philosophy and Phenomenological Research,* March, 1969, pp. 432 ff.

est sense formative of our modern era. There is an element of selectivity in adopting this approach, as indeed there must be in any study of the history of ideas. Nonetheless, there is an impressive continuity of cultural factors and intellectual concerns between our age and that one, together with a somewhat similar psychological stance, that justifies my hypothesis. In the long run, it will be vindicated by the light it sheds on the problem under consideration.

The Medieval

Concept of

Alienation

The theme of alienation is intrinsic to medieval Christian thought.[2] Two broad interpretations of this theme can be distinguished. First of all, there was alienation from God and, consequently, alienation from the order of the universe he was presumed to have created. Thus Satan was considered the prime example of the *alienus* and with him the fallen angels, demons and other iniquitous creatures, including the sinner. To sin was in a basic definition to alienate oneself from God and the providential order he laid down for man to follow. And since sin, at least insofar as it was inherited, was inevitable and the order of the world necessarily contaminated by an initial fall, alienation was taken to be fundamental.

A second kind of alienation was less radical, although

45

consequent upon the first. It concerned man as a stranger (wayfarer, pilgrim) upon earth. Medieval literature on this theme is abundant and invariably stresses the insubstantiality of all things corporeal and mundane. The Christian was often portrayed as affixed to the ark of the Church as Ulysses had been lashed to the mast of his ship in order to steer an undistracted course amidst the siren calls of the world. In another much quoted image, man was seen as a *viator* in this life, the world as an inn, death as the journey's end and heaven as his final home. Innocent III's classic *On the Misery of Man* is a lugubrious catalogue of woes that translated a deeply felt and widespread attitude of separation and unworthiness. He begins with this mournful declaration of intent: "Let me deplore the miserable beginnings of human existence; let me lament its sinful progress; let me mourn its end in damnation." And he goes on: "Human life is constant fear, trembling, horror, pain, sadness, restlessness."[3] And so forth.

The challenge to intellectual systems, on the other hand, was to try to absorb this negative religious view into an order of integrity, harmony and reconciliation. The medieval intellectual tradition (particularly Scholasticism) shared a common conviction, as David Knowles puts it, that there existed "a single reasoned and intelligible explanation of the universe on the natural level, and a single analysis of man and his powers, that could be discovered, elaborated and taught, and that this was valid for all men and final within its own sphere."[4] The macrocosmic and miscrocosmic orders were often so skillfully balanced and a hierarchical scale of being so firmly established that it often seemed (as in Aquinas' *Summa*) as though all dichotomies and oppositions were dissolved. But what we must take pains to point out is that for the medieval schoolmen there could be no adequate account of man or the world "on a natural level." Aquinas typically begins by constructing a theory of the divine personality and makes this a basis for his analysis of man. All intellectual accounts of reality had to respect the prior assumption that God was the first cause of all things and his will was the ultimate basis of morality. Thus dealienated accounts of the world were, more often than not, achieved by denying much that was in the world and forcing the latter into "unnatural" categories. O'Dea notes this peculiar characteristic of medieval thought when he writes that "one of the great ironies of our history is that Western man achieved the most impressive this-worldly accomplishments although his fundamental world-view gave him little basis for significant interpretation of his achievements." And more specifically: "While our European ancestors of the tenth and eleventh centuries worked out the solution to difficult environmental problems . . . they accepted a definition of what man should be doing here below of a pronounced other-worldly character."⁵ This radical tension marks all medieval thinking and is perhaps the principal reason why in the end the efforts toward reconciliation fell prey to those pessimistic undercurrents that denied any valid equation between the God-given and natural orders of things. As Ladner notes, from the fourteenth century onward Western Christendom "was seized by a new kind of alienation" that had not previously existed. The symbolic structure of meaning, never secure, disintegrated, leaving a void that came to be filled with the overt symptoms of mass alienation— fear, melancholy, skepticism and intense anxiety. Karl Mannheim rightly observes that the works of Bosch and Grünewald show how the disorganization of the medieval order expressed itself in a general fear and anxiety.⁶

□ THE AGE OF ALIENATION

The medieval dilemma is illustrative of a larger connection between religion and alienation. For, as Feuerbach was later to argue, religion is a projection of man's most authentic values and aspirations into an alien, transcendent realm. In his view, religion is essentially alienative. In a more recent analysis, Peter Berger adopts a somewhat similar position. "The fundamental 'recipe' of religious legitimation," he writes, "is the transformation of human products into supra or non human facticities. The humanly made world is explained in terms that deny its human production. The human nomos becomes a divine cosmos, or at any rate a reality that derives its meaning from beyond the human sphere. . . . *The essence of all alienation is the imposition of a fictitious inexorability upon the humanly constructed world.*" (My emphasis.) An intrinsic ingredient of religious experience is the worship of what totally transcends the human. Religion postulates a realm of reality that is not only beyond any scientific analysis but beyond all adequate human expression. The mystic can only weakly communicate his vision through metaphor. The vision itself is of something "other." Thus "in positing the alien over against the human, religion tends to alienate the human from itself." Berger does not go so far as to equate religion and alienation. In fact, he is careful to point out that in some important ways religion has always been an "effective bulwark against anomy" and symbolic of man's effort to make his experience meaningful. But religion is alienative in this fundamental sense that its "empirical tendency has been to falsify man's consciousness of that part of the universe shaped by his own activity, namely, the sociocultural world . . . Alienation and false consciousness always entail a severance, in consciousness, of the dialectical relationship between man and his products, that is, a denial of the fundamental socio-cultural dialectic." The religious mind cannot get a very firm understanding of the world at hand because it cannot see it clearly or, more accurately, sees it reflected and distorted through the prism of transcendent categories. The first result of this attitude is a paralysis of choice. The self is, so to speak, pried loose from its natural habitat of operation. Transformative action becomes difficult because the ground of meaning is posited in a necessary, non-human realm rather than in decision, in mystery rather than understanding. Berger's summarizing statement seems to me precise: "By means of the 'otherness' of the sacred the alienation of the humanly constructed world is ultimately ratified. Inasmuch as this inversion of the relationship between men and their world entails a denial of human choice, the encounter with the sacred is apprehended in terms of total dependence."[7]

The Augustinian Influence

The medieval world-view provides a paradigmatic instance of alienation. I want now to discuss briefly Augustine's influence on the development of this view. No figure, surely, had more influence on medieval thought. Augustine's strategic historical position enabled him to become the mediator both of the early Christian and Hellenic traditions. And in mediating them, he adjusted them to the requirements of his own psychological needs and conception of reality. One is struck first of all by the Gnostic dimension of Augustine's thought. Human nature is viewed as fundamentally bifurcated and estranged, rent by a radical dualism. To be born is to take leave of that integrated realm where truth and existence coincide. The world is in a fallen, anti-divine state, given over to demonic influences. Furthermore, this "evil world" is associated primarily with its physical and material aspects. Sexuality, power, money, —all human institutions are corrupt in their roots.

This insight controls Augustine's theory of salvation. Convinced of his unworthiness and the pervasiveness of evil, he sets out to construct a doctrine of transcendence that in the end bears only an incidental relationship to the dynamics of history, a doctrine that stresses conversion over transformation, the eternal over time and the mythological over the rational. He found in Neoplatonism a philosophy that eminently suited his purposes. It enabled him to locate the powers of creativity primarily in the deity and reduce the problem of evil that so aggravated his consciousness of man's separation from his creative ground. Salvation thus becomes an effort to reestablish contact, to undertake an inward journey to a realm of purity beyond the system of this world.

What is important to note here is the manner in which Augustine reinterprets the biblical data. Salvation is no longer a historical and transformative confrontation with the evil of the world; it becomes a mystical ascent above historical realities, thus leaving the fallen world basically unaltered. The believer endeavors to negate the evil of the world by going beyond it, which is an effective means of ignoring it. This doctrine has an important psychological advantage: it enables the believer to find a new world "above" the present one; by a gradual process of purification the self can transcend the finite and experience immediate communion with the supreme reality of God. This state of reconciliation probably cannot be sustained at great length in this world; but it constitutes an important harbinger of things to come and furnishes psychological relief from the pains of existence. Such a view of salvation is no longer continuous with the given order of nature or history since these are dominated by a cosmic evil power. Augustine posits the principle of God's dominion over against the alien and hostile principle of the world. There is, to be sure, drama in this conception of redemption. But it is no longer the historical drama of biblical revelation. Nor is it the drama of reason that is found in the naturalism of Plato or Aristotle. The power of reason, through the instrumentality of Gnosticism and Neoplatonism, has been diluted into a kind of mystical voluntarism.

This interpretation, it seems to me, is supported by Augustine's theory of knowledge. His doctrine of salvation commits him to a central dualism of body and soul. Since the soul is the superior substance, and since an inferior substance cannot influence a higher one, a serious problem of the status of the sense world is raised. This problem flows logically from any doctrine that considers man as primarily a soul using a body. "All that which is in the soul comes to it from within, all that which is in the body comes to it from the soul."[8] The senses cannot be the source of knowledge. What, then, is its origin? Augustine postulates a theory of innatism. God is the inner master, the intelligible sun, whose illumination touches the minds of all men on condition that they turn away from the corporeal, purify themselves of vices and lift their minds in contemplation of spiritual truth. A theory of knowledge of this kind effects a displacement of the *true* by the *good* and necessitates the primacy of the will, that power which respects the good. A voluntarist is capable of intense intellectual activity. But he can only seriously consider such facets of reality as can be readily harmonized with what he takes (more strictly, what he wills) to be the good. On this view, significant elements of the given must be in an a priori fashion eliminated from the purview of intelligibility. In a doctrine where God is above all eternal and immutable, the philosophical problem of the one and the many becomes the theological problem of the relation between time and eternity. As such it is fundamentally insoluble. For in this framework created things have being insofar as they derive their existence from God; in themselves they incline toward non-being. Augustine taught that matter and temporal succession are most removed from God and consequently "are nearly nothing." And just as the world came into being by a gratuitous act of God's will, so too must we must work out our destiny through a series of decisions. In a world so conceived, Lovejoy rightly points out, will is prior to intellect. It is no longer a question of what *is* but of what *ought* to be.[9]

The ethical consequences of this epistemology are far-reaching. One is especially worth noting: the mark of moral worth becomes intention rather than achievement. Provided the will is properly motivated, it doesn't actually matter what we do. Love and then do as you please, as Augustine himself put it in a much-quoted phrase. Too much concern with the substance of ethics, with ethical conduct, would be for Augustine a hubristic effort to alter what God has willed for us. Because the circumstances of our lives have been predetermined, whatever we do will be of little avail. What matters supremely is establishing the right relationship with God. His will is the ultimate basis of morality, and conformity to that will is the main business of life.[10]

In Augustine we have an explicit formulation of the misery of the human predicament that is still with us today, particularly in existentialist literature. "If I attempted to give an adequate account of these manifold disasters . . . what limit could I set?" he asks. The logic of his scheme of salvation led inevitably to his debasement of man; by attributing all perfection to God he conveniently accommodated his own pessimism. The *City of God* portrays mankind as a mass of sin. Men live lives of conflicting desires and anxiety. The earthly city is in perpetual conflict—with the good and within itself. The possibility of realizing a just life in society is impossible. Classical ethical thought regarded man as capable of *knowing* and therefore *doing* the good. Augustine's voluntarism denies the equation between intelligence and value. The *Confessions* urge an inner world upon the true believer. In the soul abide truth and God. Self-knowledge is imparted as a gift from above and is the golden pathway to communion with what is best and highest. Augustine thus divides man against himself in a way that precludes any acceptance of the whole self. By definition, disquietude is a symptom of a state of dispersion and fragmentation. To feel oneself split, torn apart and scattered is to reflect a desire for spiritual unity and meaning. But the desired unity lies beyond the power of human achievement. This diremption dramatizes both man's inner alienation and his alienation from the ambient world.

Nominalism and Alienation

Augustine gave Western thought a decisive voluntaristic twist. In so doing he found what he considered a solution to the problematic of experience, a solution which, as we have indicated, constitutes an important source of the problem of alienation. Another important source can be found in the nominalism of William of Ockham (taken here as the central figure of a broader movement). It is generally charged that Ockham sundered the world of knowing from the world of reality. This charge arises primarily in connection with his theory of knowledge according to which the knowing mind abstracts neither essence nor nature from things because it cannot be shown that either the mental process of abstraction or any nature to abstract exists. Whatever we know is individual and singular rather than general or universal, and the process of knowledge is intuitional rather than abstractive. The nominalistic concern with singulars ushered in a way of thinking that sees the world as disparate rather than continuous or interrelated. As Anton Pegis has put it: "The Ockhamist notion of science is the victim of all the atomization which the singularity of things introduces into concepts and judgments" and raises "a real conflict between demonstration and singularity." And he adds:

> Given that being is simple, or, if composite, constituted of really distinct parts; and given that in such a world there are no communities among things, either absolutely or in fact—then, failing intuition, knowledge suffers from all the ways in which it does not answer to the pure singularity of things . . . In a world of absolutely simple singulars, there is no basis in things for demonstration; for such a world offers no communities to the intellect on which it might base the relations of its concepts.[11]

The problem of universals had interested most of the medieval philosophers and theologians. In the main they arrived at realistic solutions. Ockham was by no means the first to be fascinated by the singular status of things outside the mind. Nor was he the first to propound a terminalist solution to the problem of knowledge. But his influence on the future development of thought was of enormous importance. He was one of those thinkers who "sum up and carry forward" (to use Dewey's expression) a whole cluster of cultural attitudes and concerns. What Ockham wants us to realize, Gilson points out, is that "since everything that really exists is individual, our general ideas cannot correspond to anything in reality, whence it follows necessarily that it is not their nature to be either images, or pictures, or mental presentations of any real or conceivable thing."[12] Nothing can be concluded from cognition concerning the existence or nonexistence of its object. It is not only that we do not really know any *thing* at all; more seriously, it may be that there is nothing extra-mental to know. It is true that Ockham speaks in this vein with respect to abstractive knowledge. He was not anxious to face the prospect of losing his world. Thus he made extensive use of the category of intuitive knowledge, which he defined as immediate perception of really existing things and as such the foundation of our experimental or scientific knowledge (*experimentalis notitia*). In his own words: "Nothing can be known in itself naturally save by intuitional knowledge" (I *Sent.* dist. 3, p. 2). Such knowledge is attended by a feeling of certitude. It is self-evident and (here we detect shades of Descartes' final recourse) guaranteed by God.

But the guarantee was not at all reassuring, even for Ockham. The test case was the intuition of nonexisting things. Why could not God (whose omnipotence Ockham continually stressed) sustain in us the intuition of nonexisting things? There is no reason why the world might not be a vast dream unsupported by any reality whatsoever. Ockham's razor was extremely sharp. In the end it honed the scope of knowledge down to "empirical sequences of facts outside the mind, the habitual associations within the mind, the mere external frame of a world order carefully emptied of its intelligibility."[13] The vital bond between the mind and its world is broken. Ockham secured conceptual activity as a theory of the nature and structure of knowledge and thus exacerbated a duality between thought and being, the knower and the known, the subject and the object. The kind of reciprocity, indeed intimacy, that existed between man as an intelligent knower and the world as an intelligible known in classical thought was no longer possible. Consequently, knowledge became alienated from the world together with the mind. Logically extended, this position points to a structureless world since no community of being actually exists; rather there exists only a community of signs, of mental constructs, which furnishes the universality necessary for knowledge but is unable to build any sure bridge to the extra-mental world of particular and individual things. John Herman Randall makes this comment on the outcome of nominalism:

> The fact of knowledge no longer has implications for the nature of the world that sustains it; its only implications are for man and his manner of knowing the world, whatever be its nature. . . . The structure of nature is no longer to be construed in terms of the structure of knowledge. . . . It is to be described as what it is simply observed to be. . . . Being a theory of experience rather than of what is experienced, nominalism has always proceeded from an initial realism as to the cause of experience to an experience that has for-

gotten its cause. Its fate has been in the fourteenth century, in the eighteenth and twentieth, to fall into a subjectivism from which only the most strenuous efforts have been able to extricate it. That history is an important part of modern thought.[14]

Some ethical consequences of nominalism can now be considered. To begin with, we find in Ockham a much more radical voluntarism than in Augustine and a complete rejection of the primacy of the intellect in God and man. Consistent with his theory of knowledge, Ockham held that the object of God's knowledge is particular things rather than universal ideas. Moreover, his knowledge in no way constrains his will. Rather the contrary is the case. His will suffers no constraints whatsoever. There is no order of things prior to the exercise of God's will. It follows from this that God's essence is his will, which alone is constitutive of the good for man. Further, since in his absolute autonomy God is not bound to any of his decrees, the moral order he imposes on men is only conditionally binding. If this is the case, then morality becomes virtually arbitrary, for it lacks stable grounding. As Ernest Moody states it: "If the Christian believer gives wholehearted acceptance to the doctrines of divine freedom and omnipotence, he cannot consistently suppose that there is a necessarily existential order in the created world. But if the world is out-and-out contingent, there can be no a priori reasons for its existence or for its de facto order; empiricism is thus a logical consequence of belief in the Christian doctrine of divine freedom."[15]

We have here a very peculiar instance of the alienated consciousness. Normally religion legitimizes morality by rooting it in an inexorable supra-human order. Ockham does something like the opposite. He dissolves the stable ground of morality by linking it to the arbitrary unfolding of God's unrestrained will. This is very odd and must have seemed so to Ockham, for he attempts to modify his position by arguing that in the *ordinary* exercise of his will God is consistent. But it remains true that there is no reason for this consistency. God could at any time change his mind, so to speak, and impose a different set of commands just as he could delude me into thinking I perceive some object when in fact I don't. God's omnipotence is such that by a direct act of the will he can produce any effect. Skepticism, both about natural knowledge and the moral order, would seem to be the necessary consequence of this position. Ironically enough, Ockham intended no skepticism. He objected to traditional realism because he believed it placed the ultimate reality in some supra-sensible domain and denigrated the finite world. This objection would have been given particular force within the sacramental perspective of the Middle Ages which saw the world as a mirror of a greater reality elsewhere. It seems to have been in protest against such dualism that Ockham developed his empiricism. He was motivated by a desire to map out a legitimate area for finite minds, unbothered by the intrusions of the infinite. The emphasis now falls upon the subjective rather than the supernatural. At this juncture nominalism and mysticism meet. They are, Erwin Panofsky writes, but two sides of the same coin.

> Both mysticism and nominalism cut the tie between reason and faith. But mysticism . . . does so in order to save the integrity of religious sentiment, while nominalism seeks to preserve the

integrity of rational thought and empirical observation . . . both mysticism and nominalism throw
the individual back upon the resources of private
sensory and psychological experience; *intuitus* is
a favorite term and central concept of Master
Eckhart as well as of Ockham. . . . Both mysticism
and nominalism end up with abolishing the
borderline between the finite and the infinite. But
the mystic tends to infinitize the ego because he
believes in the self-extinction of the human soul
in God, whereas the nominalist tends to infinitize
the physical world because he sees no logical contradiction in the idea of an infinite physical
universe and no longer accepts the theological
objections thereto. Small wonder that the nominalistic school of the fourteenth century anticipated the heliocentric system of Copernicus, the
geometrical analysis of Descartes, and the
mechanics of Galileo and Newton.[16]

In a perceptive essay H. Obermann notes how the dual
emphasis of nominalism—on singulars and God's omnipotence—brought about a new kind of conflict. The transcendent perspective receded from the immediate range of
men's interests and became a kind of "dome that shuts out
the world of God's nonrealized possibilities and provides
room on the inside for man's own realm in which he thinks
and acts."[17] The divine and human realms are now linked
only by a kind of terrible freedom. On nominalistic premises man's dignity is not the result of his participation in
being (or the divine nature) but of God's decision to grant
him an autonomous freedom to do with what he may.
Stress on autonomous freedom naturally accompanies any

theory that postulates the primacy of the will over the intellect. This displacement has been a constant cultural factor, from Augustine through Ockham (and, of course, a good number of other medieval thinkers), Renaissance humanism, Descartes, Rousseau and Kant, German idealism to present-day existentialism. It has, in fact, become the burden of freedom that pains all the anti-heroes of contemporary literature. Obermann also points out that sin "no longer marks the need of God's saving presence but has become naturalized as a tragic consequence of man's aloneness in this world. In nominalism it is the unpleasant, but surmountable, consequence of a decree of God which has no metaphysical ramifications." It is, to speak in a modern vein, lonely under the dome. Obermann puts it well: "In his loneliness nominalistic man is anxious to keep close to the reality of the world about him, an anxiety naturally accompanied by the secularization of his interests. . . . His newly won freedom gives him the heavy responsibility of guarding against hallucinations. He can no longer afford to keep his eyes constantly on his ultimate goal as did Augustinian man nor to trust his reason to the same extent as did Thomistic man."

A similar conclusion could be argued from the perspective of social criticism. Edward Conze, for example, has ably tried to show that nominalism, science (the chief purpose of which is to understand events in purely human terms and control nature by mechanical means), capitalism and the bourgeois class arose together during the later Middle Ages and have remained indissolubly bound together during their subsequent histories.[18] The emergence of a new economic system in conjunction with the rise of nominalism is especially striking. Conze notes that the features of nominalism which made it attractive to the bourgeois mentality were its denial of essences, its opposition to the feudal aristocracy and the principle of parsimony. By denying universals, the nominalist not only struck a blow against metaphysics and natural theology but at the same time contributed to the development of scientific method. The principle of parsimony had a particular appeal to the bourgeoisie, for it comforted them with the thought that the processes of nature respect the principles of economics. Nature was thrifty. The bourgeois view of the cosmos arose out of a direct analogy with the kind of social world they were interested in establishing.

But thrift can often be very costly. By denying man a nature, nominalism led to agonizing doubts about the meaning of life; by denying relations among things, it had to hold that they were an unorganized chaos until mind supplied the connections. Conze is quite correct when he observes that the world appears chaotic to the bourgeois because of his view of social organization. "The capitalist producer is confronted by a chaos of commodities. He finds himself involved in an unplanned economy in which production is affected by the perturbations of an unregulated market. Nowhere does he find any order in society, which might govern his action. Where there is some order in society— laws, codes, agreements and contracts—it is *he* who has brought it about."[19] The objection that the nominalist's assumption about chaos is unsupported by reality is irrelevant because for him reality is a function of the mind's ordering power. The nominalist-bourgeois argues that because his social world is artificial and more or less arbitrary, so must the cosmos also be. This kind of projection is not unusual; in fact it is altogether normal in the history of ideas. A notion like "causality" is such an example. The world was seen by the Greeks to be like the human agent:

animated, purposeful, intelligent. The natural world was anthropomorphized. Something similar takes place at the end of the Middle Ages, although in this case it would be more proper to say that the natural world was mechanomorphized. By this time the anthropomorphic analogy was reversed. The human self, originally the model for explaining the workings of inanimate nature, came now to be itself explained and controlled by the artificial laws of an increasingly mechanized society. Such a self is no longer medieval.

This reduced world signaled the beginning of a distinctively modern experience. For increasingly thinkers would reject the great chain of being. The universe could be experienced but not understood as a whole. Henceforward it became ever more difficult to organize the materials of experience organically, virtually impossible to maintain the world of knowledge and the world of reality in any kind of creative partnership. The perspective within which the world had formerly been interpreted as a meaningful unity (and even pessimistic theologies like Augustine's safeguarded the category of wholeness, albeit awkwardly) disintegrated. Experience came to be understood as a congeries of disconnected simples, losing its sacramental integrity.

A Panorama of Futility

Primitive man faced his world in fear and trembling, beset on all sides by the powers of nature and his own untamed nature. He had no models of history or tradition—in a word, no adequate cultural constructs with which to shape the raw data of experience into an ethos of harmony and unity. A stark dualism obtained between man and the outer world. Nature stood against him in unmitigated enmity. This dualism generated in primitive man a need for liberation and deliverance. His religion and art forms reflect the intensity of this need. Early deities are supra-mundane and despotic, implacable in their alien aloofness. Primitive art sought to control the relative and mutable aspects of experience in rigid, geometrical forms. It was essentially an abstraction that enabled our earliest ancestors to calm their anxieties by simulating absolute values.

Classical man, on the other hand, established a more satisfactory equation between himself and his surroundings. He domesticated the gods, overcame the uncertainty of the phenomenonal world by the power of conceptual thought and elaborated appealing theories of the good life. He was at home in his world. The rigorous dualism of primitive man has given way to a happy state of psychic balance. Whence the Greeks (taken here as typical of the classical spirit) made the principle of harmony the basis of social and individual life and the measure of aesthetic realization. We are prone to exaggerate the achievements of the Hellenic era. Nonetheless, the healthy anthropomorphism of that era marked an indisputable advance in man's progressive adjustment to his environment. The great discovery of classical man was that alienation could be overcome by deploying the energies of the spirit in a free and creative manner. His sense of the beauty and rhythm in nature corresponded to the ideals of man living excellently.

Medieval man falls far short of the classical ideal of human excellence. He is much closer to primitive man in attitude. In particular he shares with primitive man a paralyzing dualism of vision, a haunting sense of guilt and anxiety as well as a need for deliverance. Medieval man's psychic stance is reflected in Gothic architecture. When we look at a Gothic cathedral we are first of all struck by the thrust of upward movement which seems to defy the weight of the stone. The towering spires diminish one's sense of materiality. It is as though the solidity of the elements used in the construction were dematerialized, thus becoming a vehicle of nonsensuous meaning. This impression of Gothic architecture is reinforced by a consideration of the use it makes of abstract line, a technique well suited to accentuate the spiraling effort to transcend the circumstances of concrete existence and reach toward the placid pastures of the infinite. Gothic form thus translates medieval man's restive quest for deliverance from the limitations of time and space, his deep-seated yearning to escape from the neurosis of life on this earth. The intoxicating effect of the Gothic line was medieval man's way of suggesting the fullness of beatific felicity.*

We might illustrate the difference between the classical and medieval mentalities in another way, by comparing Homer and Dante. Homer's Ulysses, after many trespasses against the gods and exciting adventures on the seas, returns finally to Ithaca in a proverbial symbol of man's at-homeness in the world. Christian mythology relegated the earthly Ithaca to a heavenly realm. In so doing it broke with the

---

* In the foregoing I have followed Wilhelm Worringer. For further developments see his *Form in Gothic* (New York, Schocken Books, 1964). Worringer also draws an interesting comparison between Gothic architectural and Scholasticism. Speaking of the latter he says: "Here too is an excess of constructive subtlety without any direct objective, that is to say, without any aim of knowledge—for knowledge has already been established by the revealed truths of church and dogma; here, too, an excess of constructive subtlety serves no object but that of creating an endless activity, continuously intensified, in which the spirit loses itself as if in ecstasy. In Scholasticism, as in architecture, there is the same logical frenzy, the same methodical madness, the same rationalistic expenditure for an irrational aim" (p. 107).

spherical coziness of ancient cosmologies and gave the face of reality a Janus-like appearance. Still, the forces of alienation could be contained so long as man was assured some home, even a heavenly one. This set an appropriate and even consoling *terminus ad quem* to man's pilgrimage. With Dante this sense of at-oneness has disappeared. It is significant that, unlike the Homeric hero, Dante's Ulysses never returns to his homeland. Driven by unnamed and perhaps unnamable furies he wanders aimlessly through the measureless waters until he is smashed against the mountain of Purgatory and swallowed up by the sea. Henceforward the idea of man as a *viator,* a pilgrim on his way toward a divine order, while never entirely lost, ceased to be as effective. Increasingly, man becomes a pilgrim without a destination, an aimless wanderer, and the ideology of estrangement sharpens and intensifies.

And this comparison with classicism: "The beauty of the finite was sufficient for the inward exaltation of classical man; Gothic man, dualistically riven and therefore transcendentally disposed, could only feel the thrill of eternity in the infinite. The culmination of classical architecture lies therefore in beauty of expression, that of Gothic in strength of expression: the one speaks the language of organic being, the other the language of abstract values" (pp. 108–109).

I would be inclined to judge that Worringer's judgment of Scholasticism is too severe (for at its best it represents a significant conceptual achievement), but I am in full agreement with his judgment that Gothic form is an expression of abstract, alien values. It is quite in keeping with the medieval obsession with the otherworldly and consequent negation of the sensual. It manifests the medieval conviction of the disharmony between man and nature.

---

1. Erich Kahler, *The Tower and the Abyss* (New York, Braziller, 1957), p. 160. Kahler does not concentrate on the history of the problem, however. Rather he is interested in investigating the contemporary process of human transformation which manifests itself in diverse forms of "disruption or invalidation of the indi-

vidual." And he specifies: "What we are concerned with is precisely the breakdown of human form, dissolution of coherence and structure; not inhumanity which has existed all through history and constitutes part of the human form, but a-humanity, a phenomenon of rather recent date" (p. xiv). Kahler contends that two powerful forces in recent history have contributed to the advent of a broken world and a tragic sense of alienation: "from without, the intrusion of huge collectives with their demand for conformity and functionalization and, from within, the development of man's analytic self-searching which came to shake the foundations of his existence."

2. See Gerhart B. Ladner's article "Homo Viator: Medieval Ideas on Alienation and Order," *Speculum*, Vol. XLII (1967), pp. 233–260.

3. Innocent III, "On the Misery of Men," in *Two Views of Man*, edited by Bernard Murchland (New York, Ungar, 1966), pp. 3–51.

4. David Knowles, *"The Evolution of Medieval Thought* (New York, Vintage, 1962), p. 335.

5. Thomas O'Dea, *Alienation, Atheism and the Religious Crisis* (New York, Sheed & Ward, 1968), p. 50.

6. See Rollo May's cultural analysis of anxiety in *The Meaning of Anxiety* (New York, The Ronald Press, 1950), especially pp. 151 ff.

7. All quotations from Peter L. Berger, "Religion and Alienation" in *The Sacred Canopy* (New York, Doubleday, 1967), pp. 81–105.

8. Etienne Gilson, *History of Christian Philosophy in the Middle Ages* (New York, Random House, 1955), p. 75.

9. The gradual ascendancy of the will over the intellect is one of the most important reasons for the emergence and present centrality of the category of alienation. This is not generally pointed out by scholars. See an excellent analysis of voluntarism in Frederick A. Olafson, *Principles and Persons* (Baltimore, The Johns Hopkins Press, 1967).

Olafson observes that in the intellectualist tradition the concepts of truth and falsity are applicable to judgments of values ("Intellectualism has always insisted that the goodness or badness of a thing and the rightness and wrongness of an action are functions of the nature of that thing or action rather than our feelings about it."—p. 5) and that a natural teleology is the philosophical support for this view. The Christian thinker had difficulty maintaining both the primacy of the intellect and the doctrine that God's will is the ultimate reason for all things, including morality. Aquinas, perhaps of all medieval thinkers, most successfully defended the primacy of the intellect. On occasion Augustine took this intellectualist approach, as in his *De Ideis*. But on the whole he did not. Copleston, among others, has made this clear. In his *History of Philosophy* (New York, Doubleday, 1962), Part I, p. 97, he writes: "It is by the will that man reaches out towards God and finally takes possession of and enjoys Him . . . Augustine's ethic thus centers round the dynamism of the will." This is an altogether expected concomitant of his theory of knowledge as interior illumination.

See also Neal W. Gilbert, "The Concept of Will in Early Latin Philosophy," *Journal of the History of Philosophy*, October, 1963, pp. 17–35. Gilbert argues that the will was first given a central place in moral discourse by the Stoics, particularly Seneca. Augustine, he says, took a decisive step in recognizing an evil as well as a good will and makes the adoption of one or the other the central concern of human life.

10. See further developments on this theme in W. T. Jones, *The Medieval Mind* (New York, Harcourt, Brace & World, 1969), pp. 108 ff. Jones writes: "By urging men to be content with their unhappy lot and to look for their rewards in the other world rather than this one, Augustine furnished reactionary conservatives and all upholders of the status quo with useful arguments, as well as with the authority of his name. As for the historical Church, there is, alas, considerable warrant for Marx's gibe that religion is the opium of the people" (p. 118).

11. A. Pegis, "Some Recent Interpretations of Ockham," *Speculum*, Vol. XXII (1948), p. 457. Pegis notes that Ockham's nominalism was an effort to neutralize the philosophical determinism which he found in the Greeks and Arabs. The attack on essences and reduction of things to "impervious singulars" accomplished one part of his project. The glorification of divine omnipotence, "whose consequence in Ockham was the factualization of the order of creation," completed this effort.

12. Etienne Gilson, *The Unity of Philosophical Experience* (New York, Scribner's, 1937), pp. 67–68.

13. *Ibid.*, p. 89.

14. John Herman Randall, *The Career of Philosophy* (New York,

Columbia University Press, 1962), Vol. 1, p. 38. Randall makes a strong case for the influence of nominalism on the later emergence of British empiricism and sees a direct continuity of epistemological method.

15. Ernest A. Moody, "Empiricism and Metaphysics in Medieval Philosophy," *The Philosophical Review* (April, 1958) p. 158.

16. Erwin Panofsky, *Gothic Architecture and Scholasticism* (New York, Meridian Books, 1958), pp. 14–15.

17. H. A. Obermann, "Some Notes on the Theology of Nominalism with Attention to Its Relations to the Renaissance," *Harvard Theological Review*, Vol. LIII (1960), pp. 47–77.

18. See his suggestive article, "Social Origins of Nominalism," *Marxist Quarterly*, January–March, 1937, pp. 115–124.

19. *Ibid.*, p. 123.

The Renaissance

Angle of

Vision

The Renaissance is a veritable Rorschach blotter for anyone interested in the history of ideas.* Because it is a complex period, a time not only of rebirth but also of many important new departures in human thought, evidence can be found to support multiple points of view. My discussion here shall center on some of the ways in which Renaissance thought extends medieval man's awareness of alienation. Two points seem to me preeminent in this context. There is first of all a common emphasis on man's individuality—his freedom and autonomy. Toward the end of the thirteenth century, problems of the self began

* I do not want to become embroiled in the arduous task of setting precise dates to the Renaissance era. For the sake of convenience, let it be understood that we are referring to a period that extends approximately from 1350 to 1600.

to emerge in a new way, and this theme constitutes a crucial link between the late Middle Ages (particularly nominalism) and the Renaissance periods. As Ernst Cassirer saw, all the intellectual currents that nourish the Renaissance flow into the central problem of self-consciousness.[1] A second and related link is the manner in which Renaissance thinkers continued to give free reign to the projective tendencies of the imagination. The world was still largely considered an *opus alienum,* a theocracy whose rationality, order and unity were assigned to an ultimate spiritual principle through a succession of hierarchical schemes.

The Faith of the Humanists

Even a brief analysis of humanist writers reveals a persistent narcissism, a preoccupation with man's prerogatives and special claims to a privileged status in the universe.

> There cannot be a creature more divine
> Except (like Thee) it should be infinite.
> —Sir John Davies

In Gelli's fable *The Circe,* Ulysses says that man is the Lord of the universe and can by nature "do whatever he pleases." Petrarch, meditating on top of Mont Ventoux recommends the priority of invisible things. "The life we call blessed is located on a high peak," he says, and the spatial image conveys his conviction that the mountain on which he stands appears minuscule by comparison with the heights that could be reached by man's soul. Pico, in a passage that has become the classic embodiment of the optimism of the Renaissance humanists, argues that man has no fixed limits or forms. He is free to determine his own nature, to create *ex nihilo,* as it were. Pico has God say to man: "Thou shalt have the power, out of thy soul's judgment, to be reborn into the higher forms which are divine." Manetti, refuting the dark pessimism of Innocent III, extolls the dignity of man to great lengths. He concludes his work, *The Dignity of Man,* satisfied that he has proven "first, how great and wonderful is the dignity of the human body; secondly, how lofty and sublime the human soul; and finally, how great and illustrious is the excellence of man himself made up of these two parts." And Ficino, beaming his Neoplatonic mind over a vast panorama of ideas, pens an ennobling appreciation of the human estate. Man's soul, he writes:

> . . . bears within herself the images of the divine essences on which she depends, as the grounds and models of the lower things which she has in a certain manner created. She is the middle of all and possesses the power of all. She enters into everything, without losing a part of herself, since she is the true connection of all things, when she addresses herself to another. She may rightly be called the center of nature, the middle of the universe, the chain of the world, the countenance of all, the bond and fetter of all things.[2]

Similar passages abound in Renaissance writing.* Withal, they are a faithful, even intensified, echo of the medieval conviction that man was an *imago Dei.*

Such affirmations appear very healthy and dealienated. The principles upon which they rest were the time-honored principles of cosmic order. Reality forms a unity; the many

---

* For a broad sampling of opinion on human dignity and cosmic order among Renaissance writers see Herschel Baker, *The Image of Man* (New York, Harper Torchbooks, 1961), pp. 203 ff.

constitute a series of connected images of the One; man is the glory of creation. The Renaissance humanists were even more enamored of hierarchical structures that were medieval man and because of this were often able to get their experience into sharper focus. Castiglione's Cardinal Bembo speaks typically of the beauty and comeliness of the world: "The celestial bodies among themselves have such force by the knitting together of an order so necessarily framed that with altering them any one jot, they should be all loosed and the world would decay." Or Ficino again: "Certainly the universal motion of the cosmos in itself cannot be lacking in perfect order." Like many of his time he concluded that all things are governed by the most rational of beings. Wylie Sypher remarks upon the importance of order for Renaissance man: "The humanist concept of nature is really an assertion of a will to reconstruct man's environment from a certain angle of vision . . . The Renaissance artist-and-scientist had an abiding faith that space is strictly measurable and can be formally arranged within a cosmos, that all the constructions of art have a law of unity, harmony and coherence. The Renaissance evolved its aesthetic world from an almost Pythagorean belief that all is number; it tried to obey in both art and science a theory of quantitative relations."[3] And he adds that the reintegration of space is probably the most important aesthetic achievement of Renaissance humanism.

But there is a not altogether paradoxical sense in which the emphasis on symmetry and the buoyant idea of *uomo universale* conceal swift undercurrents of insecurity and even despair. What we have to bear in mind is that Renaissance man was keenly conscious of his divided nature, of living in a double world. On the one hand he was aware of his unlimited powers and freedom—what Symonds has described as "the epiphany of the modern spirit"— and on the other, he felt constricted by mortality and finitude. He reacted to this dilemma in basically the same way as did his medieval forbears: by reconstructing the given world in terms of imaginative ideals. This reconstruction implied both a withdrawal from the immediate world of human experience (whence the brittle, abstract character of much Renaissance output) and a tendency to exaggerate man's powers of creativity (whence the strident emphasis on human dignity). For this reason much Renaissance optimism is seen, upon closer inspection, to be predicated upon a denial of limit and a boundless hope for self-transformation. It often enough turns out to be a form of idealism that contains the seeds of its own disintegration. Alienation is closely linked with man's compulsion to pursue an unattainable goal and in attempting this hubristic ideal meets with a fall and loses his soul to the devil.[4] I would defend the view that the Renaissance humanists contributed significantly to what became known as Romanticism and saw man, as later Vico and a host of Romantics were to see him, as a finite principle tending toward the infinite: *posse, nosse, velle finitum quod tendit ad infinitum.* At bottom, such a temperament despairs of the given condition of man, the world as it is, and subjects them to radical transformation. The Romantic mind is inexhaustibly equipped with redemptive techniques. Thus Pico's God says: "The nature of all other things is limited and constrained within the bounds prescribed by me; thou, coerced by no necessity, shalt ordain for thyself the limits of thy nature in accordance with thine own free will, in whose hand I have placed thee."

Pico, in fact, is a representative case in point. He well illustrates that Renaissance awareness of the duality of experience. Man's freedom is indeterminate, without limits. This enables him to transcend the laws of causality which apply to the universe. Thus he is, as Harry Berger has argued, both here (in the world of mortal bodies) and there (in the ethereal domain of all-things-in-all-things).[5] Pico in effect, as Berger rightly notes, posits a disjunctive relationship between the world and man or, perhaps more accurately, between the world as it is and as it is imagined, and takes the latter to be the more real. This dualism does not seem to me less problematic than that of Augustine. Freedom is in both cases transcendental and ahistorical, although in Pico's scheme man is given far vaster powers to create himself. We have, as it were, the same Neoplatonic hierarchy without the Augustinian stress on evil and pre-destination. Yet the outcome is the same, for in either case we must escape the world. In either case it is love of the higher things that enables us to soar above the finite. Whether by the grace of God or, in Pico's terminology, "the grace of truth," the thrust is always upward. Withdrawal from the problems of life to engage in the experiences of contemplation thus becomes the main business of life. The soul ascends in a unilateral direction toward the infinite. This is the mark of man's special perfection: no goal can contain him; he must constantly strive and seek beyond any set limits. In Cassirer's judgment this upward movement most clearly expresses the "basic Faustian attitude of the Renaissance." The striving for the infinite, he says, "the inability to stop at anything given or attained is neither a fault nor a shortcoming of the mind; rather, it is the seal of its divine origin and of its indestructibility. We can easily follow this basic and characteristic Renaissance motif as it penetrates every sphere of intellectual endeavor and is modified in each of them. The same motif is at the center of

Leonardo's theory of art and at the center of Ficino's philosophical doctrine of immortality."[6]

This humanist conception of man directly challenged the classical emphasis upon limit and moderation and led inevitably to a separating out of human nature into what it is and what it cannot become, thus creating a finite-infinite dichotomy which confuses man's identity and exhausts his energies in a doomed effort to achieve the impossible. Man is not entitled to absolute status, nor can he spin his substance out of the pure cloth of cerebral activity. Sooner or later he must take account of the empirical and sensuous conditions of his existence. These cannot be long negated without harmful consequence. Renaissance humanists were mainly interested in defending a (more or less orthodox) religious position and consecrated their best efforts to this end. Their avid interest in classical sources went hand in hand with an attempt to draw out the implications of man's Christian birthright: his superiority and indeed isolation from the rest of the created order. It may be admitted that this was motivated by a desire to unify experience in light of the category of wholeness. But it reflected a mistaken estimate of human potential and in the end brought about that awareness of brokenness and disassociation that sets in when we realize that the world is not what we thought it was.

In both the Augustinian and Renaissance perspectives it is difficult to fit man into his world, and a dilemma is created that can only be escaped by postulating a dual world—the two cities (in Augustine's case) or the determinate world of nature and the boundless sphere of human possibilities (as in the case of the humanists). The Augustinian ethos received fresh impetus in the mystic movements of the fourteenth century (Eckhart, Tauler, Suso, Gerson and the influential *devotio moderna* school at Deventer of which Cusanus and Erasmus were two illustrious alumni) and did much to shape the outlook of Petrarch, Machiavelli, Savonarola, the Florentine Neoplatonists and other leading humanists. Their conception of man's dignity was predicated upon a more or less explicit contempt for this world or, as in the more optimistic spirits, justified in terms of a larger dialectic that gave primacy to the soul and its eventual fulfillment in an alien realm.[7]

The work of Michelangelo (d. 1564) is symbolic of the humanist effort. His early creations ("David," for example) give evidence of a robust mind, exultant and whole, and they express a sound faith in the dignity of man, the possibility of harmony and the meaningfulness of the world. Sensuality and the excellence of the spirit are happily conjoined. The human figures are powerful and coherent. But when we examine them closely, we notice marked signs of anxiety and perturbations. His later works especially (the "Pietà," "Last Judgment") become withdrawn, discordant and hesitant. They translate Michelangelo's fear, his desire to be out of the times. He seems to have despaired of the humanist hope, and the lumpish, brutish character of his later period indicates that terror is at the gates. Michelangelo's work translates the trajectory of Renaissance humanism: a bold assertion of human worth that implied its own negation.

The Rise of Science and Alienation

Parallel to the humanist movement the naturalistic bent of such figures as Pompanazzi and Zabarella at the northern Italian universities and the Ockhamist school in Paris— "the most progressive thinkers of the time"[8]—were explicating the foundations of modern science. In so doing they progressively neutralized the relevance of religious supports for scientific argument (immortality of the soul, etc.) and, paradoxically perhaps, neutralized the relevance of the world itself to human destiny. One of the first consequences of the new science was to destroy the traditional idea of the uniformity of nature. The old view of the hierarchy of perfections, each neatly dovetailing with the others to form a unified picture, was called into question. What is implied here is a collapse of the structural principles with which a world view had been put together. Under the impact of the new theories originating primarily with the Parisian school (Gregory of Rimini, John Buridan, Albert of Saxony and Nicholas of Oresme among others) and more fully put forth by Copernicus, Kepler, Bruno, Galileo and eventually Newton, there was no place for such explanatory principles as hierarchical forms, final causes, functional structures, species or spiritual forces—principles that had been held central in the traditional view. A different mode of intelligibility was introduced that was mathematical and mechanical in nature. The cosmos came to be seen as infinite and pluralistic rather than finite and uniform. From one point of view this emphasis represented yet another aspect of the Renaissance exaltation of man. The earth was elevated to cosmic status; it shared in the perfection and divinity of the stars. Man, for his part, was given a superior, if not infallible, tool of understanding in the form of mathematical symbols. The grounds of wholeness seemed at least as strong as those provided by the humanists. But considered in historical perspective, the emergence of modern science contributed to man's growing sense of alienation in several ways.

For example, the new mode of intelligibility was to create problems for man's knowledge of the world, many of which have remained insoluble to this day. Part of the difficulty stemmed from trying to reconcile the "new knowledge" with the traditional patterns of interpretation. On the one hand, the new science could hardly be squared with the Neoplatonic tradition which considered the proper object of science to be Logos, a rational system that denigrated empirical content. On the other hand, the Aristotelian tradition, holding that intelligibility is embedded in the world of experience and plurality, accorded awkwardly with the formal and autonomous claims of mathematics. Finally, if the new sciences were to be interpreted according to the nominalists as an analysis of definitions and relations (as in Newton and Locke), a real danger of subjectivism threatened.[9] Thus the materials of the new science proved intractable, and in some cases unintelligible, vis-à-vis its methodology. By formulating its principles on a mathematical model, the scientific method had to mechanize (and thus reduce) the world of man's experience. The loss of meaning thereby incurred is directly relevant to the contemporary problem of alienation.

A related difficulty was the abstract and impersonal character of scientific method. Scientific knowledge aims to construct a system of general laws in order to account for the ever-changing contents of the empirical world; it seeks a universality that is disconnected from the immediate environment. It might be said that science is not interested in things but only in the general relationships that obtain among things. At any rate, science is not concerned with those aspects of things which make them humanly interesting. The scientist, strictly speaking, adopts an alien stance toward the objects of his investigation. Concerned only with their abstractable generic qualities, he studies them in a spirit that excludes the moral dimension. This method has proven ideally effective in simplifying the objects of investigation for the purposes of mathematical manipulation. But it also foreshortens the scope and richness of human experience in serious ways.* The spectator view of reality that goes with the scientific mentality is often referred to as a form of distancing. By this is meant a technique for estranging the subject from the object. One of Renaissance man's outstanding traits was his ability to separate himself from his experience and look at it from the outside, from a neutral perspective, as though he were contemplating something not vitally related to him. The object is precisely that alien reality with which we are not involved; it is experience viewed as though it were other. The consequent separation of the knowing self from the world it knows is one of the defining characteristics of alienation.

As Cassirer again points out, as soon as man erected a boundary between himself and the world, he suffered an incurable wound of being alienated from an order that could only be thought. In this respect Renaissance man seriously modified his medieval heritage. He no longer considers sensible appearances a trustworthy guide to the truth about reality. The real is no longer embodied in the visible things of the world. The sacramental vision disappears as a new, mathematical kind of faith gains prominence. The world is now an *opus alienum* in the different sense that it becomes a construct, something refashioned and reconstituted in accordance with the mind's ideal rather than in conformity to a supposed plan for God. It is, quite literally, a fiction that has been created by the mind, which selectively controls, explores and creates the elements of reality. For the

---

*On the divorce between science and ethics, see pages 77 ff.

abstraction of supernaturalism (as reflected in Gothic art or Scholasticism) is substituted the abstraction of a different fiction, the mentally constructed world of science. From this point of view there is little to choose between science and science fiction. The inventive powers of the human mind are highlighted in both cases. This truth becomes manifest in a thinker like Descartes who projected the logic of his mind upon the world in alien and reified form. With the coming of Renaissance science, says Anton Ehrenzweig, man began to evade himself by displacing his compulsions onto the external world, where they no longer seemed to be spiritual or moral laws but laws of necessity inherent in nature.

Hannah Arendt offers an interesting analysis of the collapse of a world-view implied in the rise of modern science.* Science, she argues, introduced a unique form of alienation because, when the universe is viewed through the telescope and other high-powered instruments, its secrets are revealed with compelling immediacy. When these deliverances are further subjected to mathematical control (and modern physics frees man from the limitations of earthbound geometry), the nominalist dome recedes into the dim recesses of cosmic space and generates fear in men's hearts. Man comes from a warm womb and had been traditionally accustomed to a cozy cosmos. After the discoveries of the sixteenth century he was to be deprived of the latter luxury. (Is it only a matter of time before he is deprived of the former as well?) Arendt notes that the immediate philosophical reaction to the new vistas opened out was rampant skepticism and eventually Cartesian doubt. Sense knowledge and the world at hand yielded only minor certitude

---

* This collapse was most dramatically symbolized in the trial of Galileo.

when compared with the adequacy of our measuring instruments, the reliability of conceptual relationships reinforced by mathematical argument, and the magnificence of the infinite universe that Bruno extolled. Thus anxiety and a sense of triumph were bound up in the same event. "Whatever we do today in physics," Arendt writes, "we always handle nature from a point in the universe outside the earth. And even at the risk of endangering the natural life process we expose the earth to universal cosmic forces alien to nature's household." And she concludes: "World alienation, and not self-alienation as Marx thought, has been the hallmark of the modern age."[10] Or, as Copernicus put it: "The earth conceives from the sun, the sun rules the family of stars."

This is in some respects a curious interpretation. Arendt alerts us to a distinction of considerable importance. World alienation does indeed seem to take precedence over self-alienation as a characteristic of the modern age. But her account of why this should be the case is wanting. A natural question occurs: Why should cosmic forces be alien to nature's household? Is not the cosmos part of nature? No doubt the abstractive, reifying way in which science handles nature is part of the problem here. More deeply, I would surmise, the cosmos can be considered alien only on the prior basis that physical reality as such is suspect. Modern science, after all, emerged from and built upon a profoundly dualistic tradition. The Ockhamists, we may agree, were intellectually correct in what they tried to do but were psychologically unprepared to relish their task. They seemed unable to detach themselves emotionally from the traditional perspective of faith and did not really overcome the paralyzing dualism of that tradition. Science inherited something of that divided attitude. In this context, it is interesting to note how nominalism reaches back to join forces with Augustine's voluntarism and at the same time, by laying the foundations of modern science, stretches ahead to reinforce the abstract character of scientific thinking. In both cases there is a failure to unify experience, leaving an aggravating dualism to gnaw at the heart of man's creative efforts. In both cases truth remains double and experience divided.

The Testimony of Art

Renaissance art offers further evidence of the period's proclivity to fictionalize experience. In an excellent study of the relationship between art and alienation, Paul LaPorte observes how pre-Renaissance art (with few exceptions) was functionally integrated into the flow of man's ordinary experience. Art was meaningful to people because both appeared in a "common field of action."[11] Renaissance painters substituted perspective for this common field and addressed the individual rather than the community, in the process placing man outside of the work, making him an alien spectator, as it were. The work of art was in some literal sense abstracted from what had been its functional context. In LaPorte's words: "The emancipated work of art, independent of a specific use and context, is the most characteristic and prominent creation of the Renaissance. Its prototype is the framed easel painting. The frame symbolizes its separation from the ordinary world and the fact that it is portable contributes to its homelessness . . . The rigorous mathematics of perspective and the consequent illusion of volume and deep space are the symptoms of this development."[12]

82

In this sense, painting and science spring from a common parentage; both re-create the deliverances of the senses according to some mathematical scheme. Holding the mirror up to nature meant, for both scientist and artist, reproducing nature in accordance with a predetermined perspective. As LaPorte puts it, post-Renaissance painting "implied an observer frozen to a certain point in space, located at a certain distance from the subject, capable of encompassing but a limited area of what presented itself to his view. The rules according to which visual appearance could be projected on a plane were of a truly theoretical, scientific nature. They represent . . . a mathematical rationalization of a selected number of sense data. The relation of the artist to his subject is reduced to a science of optical mechanics mathematically formulated."[13] This tendency to "otherate" experience is altogether consistent with Western man's general inclination to self-deification. It seems each time he has come upon a technique for exploring reality— whether reason, theology, science or technology—he has used it as a means of alienation. How many times has he created an abstraction only to worship it?

The problem with perspective, or any mathematical method for that matter, and what makes it inevitably alienating is its exclusive nature. It involves the curious psychological feat of putting ourselves outside of the experience we wish to explore and then investigating only those aspects of it which accord with our a priori construct. Plato was aware of this danger of mathematics, which is why he recommended the higher method of dialectic. He had learned from Socrates that dialectic is always open-ended; it never clamps down inexorably on its subject matter. It is a way of circling a problem of investigation to understand it, i.e., to see all sides of the problem but never to lose sight of the context of the inquiry or its intimate relevance to the questioner. Perhaps this is why Plato so often let dialectic take flight on the wings of metaphor (whether poetic or mystic or religious), for metaphor is an excellent way to integrate the manifold aspects of experience that are delivered in dialectical inquiry. Mathematics furnishes a harsher technique, at once more precise and less comprehensive. Like the doorman of an exclusive club, it rejects all claims to knowledge except those bearing the purest of credentials. When perception is thus monitored by perspective a fragmented world of experience is the necessary consequence. The price for the clarity gained by breaking reality into atomic simples was the disassociation of sensibility that Eliot so rightly detected in seventeenth-century poetry. Authentic existence then became a question that has haunted the Western mind in a special way.

The doctrine of perspectivity sanctioned the Renaissance sense of individuality and made reality a function of one's point of view. In many ways this better honored the richness and plurality of experience than did traditional monisms or dualisms. The emphasis on perspective denies the validity of any universal truth; what becomes important now is the angle (or construct) that furnishes a window upon the world. The multiplicity of perspectives respects the infinitely faceted nature of reality. This is all to the good since, as Ortega y Gasset points out, a reality that remained the same from whatever point of view it was observed would be a ridiculous conception. But the price we pay for this gain is a curtailed conception of what truth is. If all perspectives are equally true, how is experience to be unified? The doctrine of perspectivity raises serious epistemological questions: What is reality? What is the world like, apart from its reflection in our consciousness? And how does the self relate to this world? No two minds see the same reality in exactly the same way; no two impressions of reality are identical. Charles Glicksberg calls attention to the alienative possibilities inherent in this position. While it effectively disposes of abstract systems of thought, he writes, "it seems to leave the human adventurer in search of reality nowhere . . . Reality becomes problematical, the self of man is lost in a semantic smog, truth is unattainable, reason is bankrupt, human knowledge a subjective distortion."[14] All too often this is indeed what happens: the way the mind sees things is the way things are.

Because Renaissance art is a function of an a priori construct rather than a vital link in the world of lived experience, it tends to become, as LaPorte correctly observes, "a mere transcendental object" and loses its basic reference to the world. It spirals away from its empirical context in a unidirectional fashion like a Gothic tower, etherizing its material components as it goes, until finally it is no more than an abstraction, suspended in lonely isolation outside of any existential matrix. What can such an object mean? Literally nothing. Its existence is inauthentic in the sense that it has left its meaning behind it. LaPorte's analysis is shrewd. "Whereas all other art tries to make the transcendent immanent, the Renaissance tried to discover the transcendent in the immanent . . . The structure of Renaissance painting makes it into something whose meaning is outside our world, something that can be experienced only by somebody who accepts its premise of projection or reflection—the very opposite of being."[15] Insofar as Renaissance humanism in general shares this abstractive tendency, what might be called a fetishism for mathematical perspective, it is a cruelly ironic humanism, separating man from his world and reducing him to an onlooker. As has been suggested, post-Renaissance man becomes, in all of his important creative endeavors, a voyeur.* Be this as it may, it can be said with much truth that the pervasiveness of alienation in contemporary society finds a distinctive antecedent in the Renaissance imagination.

The Windmills of Absurdity

Evidence of diremptive processes is abundant in late-Renaissance cultural expressions. Things began to fall to pieces. As John Donne put it, "the world's proportion disfigured is." Wylie Sypher has cogently described this period under the rubric of Mannerism—which he defines as a formal dissolution of the Renaissance style that was founded on the concept of attunement. "When we try to date this phase of instability in the arts," he writes, "we find that Mannerism appears hard upon the high-Renaissance as a sign of irresolution, a movement deprived of the sense of security, equilibrium, unity, and proportion expressed in Renaissance style."[16] It was a spasmic time, full of malaise and foreboding as portrayed, for example, in the dark world of Shakespeare's later tragedies.

Perhaps the primary manifestation of the crisis that came over Europe at this time is to be found in the religious

---

*The theme of voyeurism in contemporary fiction deserves fuller treatment in connection with the problem of alienation along the lines of Lucien Goldmann's analysis of the theme in the novels of Robbe-Grillet. Voyeurism, he says, is directly related to the transformation of person-object relationships in contemporary society. We witness on the one hand a progressive dissolution of character (in the sense that men have little control over their lives) and on the other the increasing autonomy of objects. Voyeurism thus translates man's passivity, his lack of active participation in social life and his increasing servitude to objects. It is symptomatic of the reified character of the human universe.

crisis that brought about the Reformation and the ensuing religious wars. Two observations are in order here. First of all, the Reformation drew upon the Augustinian tradition to emphasize the primacy of subjectivity, of intense personal experience. Randall offers a concise commentary on the historical importance of this stress:

> The Protestant emphasis on the individual was to make experience for the first time not the common and objective pathway by which every man might reach the world, but something private and individual. As science built on the public and open experience of the Aristotelians, so the moral philosophies of Protestantism built on this new private and personal experience. The German tradition was thus fixed as an Augustinian position suffused with Innerlichkeit, and the British as an Ockhamism made relativistic and subjective. And when science entered to remake the intellectual world, both were forced still further inward. With no remaining locus in the mechanistic world, they took up a permanent abode in individual experience, bringing all the values with them into the soul. Thus the Augustinian inwardness of the Protestants combined with the Augustinian skepticism of the French humanists to prepare the ground for that dualism between the world and human experience which Cartesian mechanics was to consummate and Newton to endorse.[17]

Secondly, by so strongly emphasizing the subjective, the reformers raised by implication serious questions concerning the basis for any knowledge whatsoever, thus contributing to the wave of skepticism that reached a climax in Neo-Pyrrhonism and made the criterion of certainty a dominant concern for philosophy ever since.

The works of the Greek skeptic Sextus Empiricus were translated in the sixteenth century. Among those most influenced by him was Michel de Montaigne, whose *Apology for Raymond Sebond* (1580) gives one of the fullest expressions to the spirit of doubt and malaise that beset that troubled time. Reading Sextus Empiricus plunged Montaigne into a skeptical crisis from which he emerged doubting all claims to knowledge based on either man's senses or reasoning capacities. Man's hubris is to believe that he can understand the world. One of Montaigne's tactics is to compare humans unfavorably with animals. Rationality is merely a form of animal behavior that is not guided by the sure instincts of the beasts. This premise could, of course, be used in defense of religion and frequently in the course of his essay Montaigne seems to adopt a fideist position in religious matters. A state of willful ignorance, he says, is an asset because it best disposes us to unquestioning belief in God's will as revealed through the institutional Church. It often seems that Montaigne is being satirical when he speaks in this vein, but there is no doubt that a conviction of skepticism led many to embrace fideism. Montaigne appears more interested in drawing out all the consequences of a strict Pyrrhonist position. He concludes that none of our faculties gives us any reliable information about the world. Even probable knowledge is ruled out. Montaigne was one of the first cultural relativists, pointing out that what is accepted as true by one culture is very often rejected as false by another. He also noted that the common beliefs about human nature prevalent in Europe were shaken by the discovery of the New World. Nor was he impressed by the achievements of the scientists who could never agree among themselves. The cumulative effect of Montaigne's arguments is powerful. We are left with the realization that reality may be no more than an insubstantial dream, unknown and unknowable against the background of a world in a perpetual state of dissolution.

Among the many literary testimonials to the Mannerist awareness of disintegration, I find Cervantes' *Don Quixote* one of the most illustrative. George Lukacs has advanced the intriguing thesis that the novel form preeminently deals with the fate of alienated man; it records the history of characters overwhelmed by the problems of existence. There is an insurmountable rupture between the novelistic hero and his world. The search for authentic values in an exploitive society, says Lukacs, constitutes the specific content of the novel genre. It is, moveover, a search that is doomed *ab initio* to failure. Consequently, an air of desperate madness, of what might be described as a futile idealism that borders on depravity, permeates the novelistic world. Such, indeed, is manifestly the case with the man from La Mancha. Cervantes, who interestingly enough died in the same year as Shakespeare, witnessed in his own lifetime the climax and downfall of Spain's position of leadership among European nations. It was a concrete instance of the prevalent turmoil. In the preface to *Don Quixote* he says that his novel is the child of disturbance, engendered in a dismal prison. That is literally true since he began to write it while serving a prison term in Seville. But it clearly has a much broader reference. The dismal prison is the world that does not respond to man's purposes, an evil world indifferent to the claims of the chivalric ideal. Like Descartes, Cervantes is convinced that some evil demon constantly conspires against him. Such a world must be subjected to radical transformation; the evil demons must be vanquished by willful striving. Alonso Quixano prepares for his conquest in a symbolic act of conversion: he renames himself and his steed, reorients his life goals and imagines unto himself a fair lady, Dulcinea del Toboso by name. He thus distances himself from the real circumstances of life and like an actor plays out a role in the imaginary theater of his mind. For Quixote the real requires no empirical content. His hope is that illusion will carry him far. Thus on his first adventure a humble inn becomes a great castle; the meager fare becomes a repast fit for a gourmet; his peasant attendants are transformed into fairy princesses. The great windmills stand for all the absurdity of the world.

Don Quixote's triumph, says Unamuno, was "a triumph of daring, not of succeeding." But if that is the case it was an ironic triumph. For a major point of the novel is that Quixote's daring changes nothing in the world. The attempt to cope with reality in purely abstract terms is futile. An infected imagination only falsifies reality. This is indicated on the physical level by the extensive abuse Don Quixote's body suffers until, beaten and bleeding, he finally comes to terms with his destructive voluntarism. None of the many inns visited in the course of the narrative are ever resting places for either his body or spirit. And so in the end, Don Quixote realizes that his way was not the right one. Will power uninformed by an intelligent consideration of the circumstances in which freedom must operate is mere vanity. Nothing really happens in the novel. Like K. in Kafka's *The Castle,* Quixote is at the end exactly where he was in the beginning. On his deathbed he reverts to his original identity. The spell of madness has been lifted; he now sees that "there are no birds in last year's nest." Ironically Sancho, who has been in the main a realistic foil to quixotism, now wishes to embark upon the same foolish quest, denying sanity to pursue the impossible dream that bestows immortality.

The period we have just analyzed represents a decisive moment in Western man's development. Post-Renaissance man does not share the vision of his forebears in which an inner-connected world system guaranteed unity and wholeness. His odyssey began, and continues painfully in the twentieth century, under the aegis of a painful dilemma: the inner man who has burned his bridges to the outer world, and an outer world that has no kinship with the inner man. Our literature is not inspired by the memory of Odysseus, adventurous yet homeward bound, but by many Hamlets and Lears hovering on the brink of self-destruction and forlornly bewailing a disintegrating order. This, in briefest formulation, is the problem of alienation as it has dominated modern thought. Post-Renaissance man "has been irrevocably cast out . . . of a childlike world of enchantment and undividedness. Since the days of his exile . . . he has been wandering in the world. Wherever he goes he is readily recognized since he bears the burden for all to see— the burden of selfhood. The ego is at once his sign of Cain and his crown of glory."[18]

---

1. Ernst Cassirer, *The Individual and the Cosmos in Renaissance Philosophy* (New York, Harper Torchbooks, 1963), p. 132. Compare Raymond Williams, *The Long Revolution* (New York, Harper, 1963), pp. 73–74. Individual, he says, meant "inseparable" in medieval thinking. "The crucial history of the modern description is a change in emphasis which enabled us to think of 'the individual' as a kind of absolute, without immediate reference, by the very structure of the term, to the group

of which he is a member . . . Slowly and with many ambiguities, we have learned to think of 'the individual in his own right,' whereas previously to describe an individual was to give an example of the group of which he was a member, and so to offer a particular description of that group and of the relationships within it." The positive aspects of the sense of individual worth that emerged in the Renaissance have often been noted, but the negative aspects, which are of direct relevance to any study of alienation, have been less so. Rollo May, one of whose dominant concerns has been to study the historical dimension of anxiety-creating cultural patterns, singles out the following negative features of Renaissance individualism: (1) its essential competitive nature; (2) the emphasis on individual power against communal values; (3) the beginnings of the equation between individual worth and material success so prevalent in our own culture; and (4) the interpersonal isolation and anxiety that flowed from these developments. (See his *The Meaning of Anxiety*, p. 165.)

2. Quoted by John Herman Randall, Jr., *op. cit.*, p. 59.
3. Wylie Sypher, *Four Stages of Renaissance Style* (New York, Doubleday, 1956), pp. 60–61, 70.
4. The history of thought shows a recurrent connection between idealism and alienation. See Lewis Feuer, "What is Alienation? The Career of a Concept," in *Sociology on Trial*, edited by Maurice Stein and A. Vidich (Englewood Cliffs, Prentice Hall, 1963), p. 130. Also, the literature of the devil's pact is a common one in the literature of alienation. See, for example, "The Alienated Person in Literature," by Bella S. Van Bark, *The American Journal of Psychoanalysis*, Vol. xxxi (1961), p. 183.
5. Harry Berger, Jr., "Pico and Neoplatonist Idealism: Philosophy as Escape," *The Centennial Review*, 13 (1969), pp. 38–83.
6. E. Cassirer, *op cit.*, p. 69. Cassirer ably shows that the idealism of modern philosophy is continuous with the basic presuppositions of Renaissance thought.
7. On Renaissance Augustinianism see P. O. Kristeller, *Renaissance Thought* (New York, Harper, 1961), pp. 82 ff.
8. Ralph Balke, Curt Ducasse and Edward Madden, *Theories of Scientific Method: The Renaissance Through the Nineteenth Century* (Seattle, The University of Washington Press, 1960), p. 3. The authors offer a convincing demonstration of the connection between Ockhamism and the later contributions of

Galileo, Descartes, Cavalieri, Torricelli, Fermat and Pascal. "Galileo and his contemporaries used the mathematical skill they had obtained in their studies of the ancient geometers to explicate and make more precise a mechanical science of which the Christian Middle Ages, in one of its aspects, had provided the most fundamental concepts and principles" (p. 4).

9. For further developments see Randall, *op. cit.*, especially the chapter on "Patterns of Interpretation," pp. 363 ff.

10. Hannah Arendt, *The Human Condition: A Study of the Central Dilemmas Facing Modern Man* (New York, Doubleday, 1959), pp. 237–38.

11. Paul M. LaPorte, "Art and Alienation," *The Centennial Review*, 12 (1968), pp. 145 ff.

12. *Ibid.*, pp. 145–147.

13. *Ibid.*, p. 148.

14. Charles Glicksberg, *The Ironic Vision in Modern Literature* (The Hague, Martinus Nijhoff, 1969), pp. 142–43.

15. Paul M. LaPorte, *op. cit.*, p. 159.

16. Wylie Sypher, *op. cit.*, p. 102. Two other very helpful studies of this period of breakdown are Hiram Haydn, *The Counter-Renaissance* (New York, Grove Press, 1960) and Marjorie Nicholson, *The Breaking of the Circle* (Evanston, Northwestern University Press, 1950). Haydn, for example, remarks of the destructive modes of thought during the Renaissance: "What unites these otherwise dissimilar thinkers of the sixteenth century is that they completely share an anti-intellectualistic, anti-moralistic, anti-synthetic, anti-authoritarian bias" (p. xiv).

17. John Herman Randall, Jr., *op. cit.*, p. 109.

18. H. Nelson and C. Trinkhaus, "Introduction," *The Civilization of the Renaissance in Italy*, by Jacob Burckhardt, Vol. I (New York, Harper, 1958), pp. 18–19.

The Rationalist

Stopgap

René Descartes and John Locke were the first important thinkers in the modern era to wrestle with the Renaissance heritage. Broadly speaking, they faced a twofold challenge. On the one hand, they were obliged to integrate the methods and discoveries of the new science within a coherent body of philosophical knowledge. Secondly, it fell to them to deal at some length with the problems of the self and its relations to the external world. With them, for the first time in the history of philosophy, the question of self-identity becomes a major preoccupation. Their response to this double challenge constitutes an important chapter in the history of alienation.

Methodical Doubt and the Alienated Self

In the context we have elaborated, Descartes' reputation as the first modern philosopher finds an added justification. He rather than Hegel (as is commonly assumed) first made the alienation of man central to philosophy. He was, so to speak, the spokesman for an era that was quite literally

94

world-less. His importance is in large measure due to the fact that his thought developed at a historical juncture where the old world of meaning had disappeared and no new meanings had yet been created. The late-Renaissance mix of old myths, emergent science and skeptical humanism formed the immediate background of Descartes' philosophy, but it provided him with no firm lever of integration. The world seemed an insubstantial pageant. This is no doubt one of the principal reasons why Descartes' thought did not develop in a context of rich empirical experience. He began by doubting all—severing every connection with materiality, authority and past experiences—and sought certainty in the mind. In so doing, he decisively transferred the emphasis of Western philosophy from a concern with the world in itself to a concern with the possibility of our knowing the world. In Professor Molina's words: "Since his time the world is no longer the object of a presupposition but, at best, the conclusion of a debate and, at worst, a fact forever beyond the human ken."[1]

Methodical doubt may be regarded as the birthmark of the alienated self. If we read Descartes as a philosophical expression of alienation the cluster of problems he bequeathed us makes more sense. These problems remain insoluble, but nonetheless they fall into a more intelligible historical perspective. Cartesian doubt is clearly more than a technique for guarding against illusions; it is more than a methodology for overcoming skepticism (although Descartes wanted to do that). It was much more thoroughgoing and occupies a place in Descartes' system, and in modern thought generally, comparable to the classical sense of wonder, *thaumazein*. Whereas the best efforts of the tradition, inspired by wonder, reached for a vision of the whole, philosophy since Descartes (if a general statement may be permitted us) has consisted of multiple ramifications and refined versions of doubting. Whence even our modern usage of the expression "I wonder" means "I doubt it." Our spontaneous intellectual reactions are toward criticism of any form of the given (and this would seem to be truer today than it was in the seventeenth century). We have become, following Descartes, demolition experts.

In some important respects Descartes prefigures the Romantic hero wandering lonely as a cloud in pursuit of some elusive fulfillment. He is never rooted to any particular set of circumstances. He worries about his status with the theologians, travels about restlessly (serving in three different armies), and eventually retires to Holland where life was "as in the remotest desert." It was on a cold day in November 1619, while he was curled up inside a large Bavarian stove (surely a withdrawal symptom) when he made his great discovery and became convinced of the universal validity of mathematical thinking—that the order of things is of the same nature as the terms of a mathematical deduction. Descartes shares with the Romantic temperament a profound dissatisfaction with the conditions of life. The real world of the sense-bound and historically conditioned mortal must be dissolved so the mind can erect its Xanadu of certainty and inwardness. This ambition was to a considerable extent motivated by Descartes' scientific ambitions. More deeply, I think, it was the outcome of his radical other-worldly dispositions. Jean-Marc LaPorte speaks of the "ascetical" dimension of Descartes' method which, he says, is "centered around a vow of poverty which renounced all the obvious and vivid certitudes of the ordinary practical pattern of experience."[2] He views the usual undertakings of men as vain in the extreme. Most of what he had learned he rejected as so much straw. He condemned the accumulated experience and wisdom of his forerunners.

Only mathematics held any appeal for him. Yet even this was unsteady and could be doubted, for the world might be the incidental plaything of an evil demon. The book of the world, the deliverances of experience, paled by comparison to "study within myself." Descartes set about "rebuilding his lodgings" single-handed, and his effort is tainted with the vulgar dualisms, ruinous tensions and deadly ambiguities (which Erich Heller saw in the later Romantics) of a mind that fears that the reality of the world may be at bottom hallucinatory.

Erwin Straus has given us a useful analysis of Descartes' philosophy in precisely this connection. In his study of hallucinations he argues that the universal application of mathematical method constitutes a serious distortion of reality and misconceives the complexity of experience. Descartes's mind-body dualism was not orginal in itself nor were most of his other categories. However, he made a very special use of them that was to have far-reaching consequences. Whereas, for example, the mind-body dualism had been traditionally paliated by seeing body and soul as cooperative functions of the experiencing creature (at least provisionally), Descartes' methodology led him to give them contradictory roles. *Res extensa,* the body, he identified with physical nature; *Res cogitans,* the thinking self, could not be fitted into nature at all. Consciousness becomes the inward arena of introspection. Straus points out that the Cartesian self is "worldless, bodyless, incorporeal and extra-mundane." And he draws this conclusion:

> The Cartesian dichotomy, therefore, not only separates mind from body, but severs the experiencing creature from nature, the ego from the world, sensation from motion. It also separates one person from another, me from you. The

> Cartesian ego, looking at the outside world, has no contact, no direct communication with any other ego . . . The outside world is never directly accessible to us. This means that reality is reached only by inference, or by deduction or projection. Reality becomes a function of judgment . . . In other words, the prelogical sphere of the immediate experience of reality has been eliminated— a tremendous loss for psychiatry, because most psychotic experiences, such as hallucinations and delusions, belong to this very realm.[3]

Descartes furnished us with an account of reality in which the parts do not fit together and indeed one in which significant features are omitted altogether.

This peculiarity of Descartes' philosophy is rather obvious and many critics have called attention to it. Most recently, Gilbert Ryle has exorcized the "ghost in the machine." But we must bear in mind that Descartes has been frequently exorcized and the ghost—that disembodied ego inhabiting a body—continues to haunt us. For we too have serious doubts about the reality of the world. Descartes' method is, therefore, still compelling for many contemporary thinkers and writers.* For, to put it as simply as possible, it is a method that enables one to cope with the world's ambiguity.

---

* For example, Husserl in his *Cartesian Meditations* hails Descartes as a predecessor of his own transcendental phenomenology which he calls a "neo-Cartesianism." Sartre avows that the beginning of his existentialism is Cartesian subjectivity. "There can be no other truth to take off from than this: I think, therefore I exist." And in his essay entitled "Cartesian Freedom," he admires Descartes for "having followed to the very end the demands of the idea of autonomy and for having understood that the sole foundation of being is freedom." It is easy to see how modern writers like Joyce, Kafka and Beckett (to say nothing of surrealism in painting) forge links with Descartes at many junctures. Beckett, in particular, vividly dramatizes the Cartesian definition of man as "a thing that thinks." His early poem, *Whoroscope*, has Descartes as the central figure.

Descartes operates fully within the Renaissance conviction that the models for the exploration of reality must be mind-made constructs rather than based on the evidence of sense experience (so too, in his own way, does Pascal). As a mathematician, he was quick to see that the geometrical method of deduction is the surest model possible. He regarded the Cogito as an axiom from which certain theorems could be deduced. His system thus possessed powerful internal coherence, untainted by sense knowledge. Descartes' eventual philosophy as it is expressed in the *Meditations* grew out of long years of effort to simplify our knowledge of physical things. He became convinced that if all the problems of physics could be solved by means of mathematics (with its purity, clarity and distinctness), there would then be no need of direct contact with the sensuously given world. But the reduction of physical concepts to movement and extension required a real distinction between mind and body. Once this is secured Descartes is in a position to affirm that the content of thought is valid without any material or sensible element. If the mind could elaborate the foundations of all certain knowledge without going out of itself, the scholastics and skeptics would be confounded and the "new science" vindicated. This, to my mind, explains the specific originality of the *Meditations*: they are inherently oriented to a duality of mind and body and the submission of the latter to explanation by mechanical principles. Descartes thus gives the dualism of mind and matter, which had been part of the Christian tradition, scientific grounding. The mind remains free while bodily things as material are determined. By means of the methodical doubt, the Cogito, clear and distinct ideas and the existence of God to confirm the otherness of the world, Descartes made his way steadily to his fundamental thesis which is found in the sixth meditation. "All that I have said about God and about truth in the third, fourth and fifth Meditations serves to further the conclusion as to the real distinction between mind and body, which is finally completed in Meditation VI."

In this way philosophy became for Descartes an enterprise of inspecting mental contents. What men now have in common is not the world of shared experience but the structure of their minds, subjective states. And these, strictly speaking, cannot be shared at all. The Cartesian revolution, as Whitehead has remarked, is based on the implicit assumption that the mind can only know what it has itself produced and in some sense retains within itself.[4] This is what he calls the fallacy of misplaced concreteness. In other words, Descartes' position regarding the perceived world is that all we really have are our perceptions. But, as Professor Molina again puts it: "The status of the perceived world remains unchanged. The real world remains outside of our awareness. Our ideas and perceptions are only links connecting our awareness with the world. Strictly speaking, for Descartes we are not aware of the world. And since the mind has no need of place, it cannot be really be said that we are in the world."[5] Cognitive activity brooks no interference as it plays out its solitary logic. Thus, when Descartes establishes what he takes to be a firm Archimedean lever in the *Cogito ergo sum,* we have the impression that a mountain has brought forth a mole. As a generalized formulation of methodical doubt it merely tells us that Descartes is a successful doubter and ends, if pushed far enough, in the solipsism of the present. From this point of view, the problem with the proofs for the good God's existence is not so much that they are circular as that they are irrelevant.*

---

*It is even possible that Descartes was an atheist. If this is so, then the elaborate role he assigns to God in the *Meditations* would be so much window dressing.

Koyré's judgment seems a fair one:

> Now it is on the basis of the clear and distinct
> ideas of our mind that Descartes has banished
> from the real world—the world as it is in itself,
> independently of ourselves and of our reason—all
> sensible quality, all "form" and all "force"—in
> short everything that is not mechanical, and has
> declared them mere appearances. He has thus
> destroyed the well-ordered, rich and colorful cos-
> mos of ancient and medieval science, substituting
> for it a new image or conception of the universe,
> mere extension and motion, an image more
> strange and much more incredible than all the
> fables ever imagined by the philosophers.[6]

When thinking is reduced to mathematical constructs, all
real connections with the world are replaced by the logical
relationships between man-made symbols. It is this reduction, as Arendt observes, that enables modern science to
"produce" the phenomena it wishes to observe.

Descartes offers a method for acquiring certain knowledge. But what, in the end, do we know? Bourdin told
Descartes that his method may keep us from error but it
will also keep us from knowing. The Cartesian odyssey
from complete doubt through the Cogito to a divine author
is an imposing *tour de force*. One might safely wager that
Descartes' *Discourse on Method* and *Meditations* will, like
the ontological argument and Berkeley's idealism, fascinate
thinkers for some time to come—not so much because
they are true as because they are "clever" and, more important, give expression to man's painful awareness of alienation in this era of history. They are, by the same token,
congenial to Western man's proclivity for playing games
with the divinity. But the time of dealienation will begin

only when we cease taking such fancies seriously. With respect to Descartes, Popkin notes: "The road from doubt, to the Cogito, to objective reality may have been the final closing of a trap which shuts us off from all knowledge save that of our own existence, and leaves us forever at the mercy of an omnipotent fiend who wants us to err at all times and in all places." For, irony of ironies, it may have been the evil demon who supplied Descartes with his clear and distinct ideas. Neither God nor mathematical certainty is immune from radical doubt.

> As long as we try to reason from our ideas to things, we will be trapped in a *crise pyrrhonienne*. All we will be able to do is reiterate over and over again that we think our ideas are true of reality, that we believe this completely, but we will never be able to assert more than that it seems to us to be the case that what we perceive clearly and distinctly is true about reality. Whether it *is* so, will forever remain a mystery . . . In Descartes' effort and failure to solve the *crise pyrrhonienne* lay one of the crucial issues of modern thought. The Reformation controversy had opened a Pandora's box in seeking the foundations of certain knowledge. The revival of Greek skepticism, the rediscovery of Sextus Empiricus, had collided with the quest for certainty."[7]

Reductionism is the worm that gnaws at the heart of the modern consciousness. And some form of reduction is implied in all types of alienation. In extreme cases it points to irrationality and signals reason's inability to encompass reality in its formulae of intelligibility. A reduced world is an absurd world—the denizens of which have been so dramatically portrayed for us in contemporary literature. Karsten Harries argues, and I think rightly, that what is at stake in Descartes' philosophy is the ontological status of the world itself and, consequently, the meaning of human existence. By reducing the world to *res extensa,* Descartes made it an object-thing *for* the subject (and here we catch a hint of the later dualism in Hegel and Sartre between the *en soi* and *pour soi* as well as the Kantian "thing in itself"). Things become the objects of a disembodied mind and the resultant subject-object dichotomy defies mediation. Harries writes:

> Implicit in this reduction is the priority of the subject over the world. Man denies himself as a member of a larger order in which he occupies his proper place. Man is no longer assigned his vocation by his place in the order of being. Indeed it is no longer possible to speak of such a place: as the being for whom the world is, man transcends and loses his roots in the world. In the course of the transformation of caring consciousness in the world into subjectivity to which objectivity is present, the world loses all meaning. . . . To operate totally within the Cartesian reduction is to pay the price of a loss of meaning and value. In the course of the reduction, being is thoroughly objectified; but objects are transcended by the subject. This makes it impossible for objects to have a claim on the subject. It is thus possible to interpret the Cartesian reduction as a step toward nihilism.[8]

To put this in a slightly different fashion, we may say that Descartes' effort to prove his existence by the fact that he thinks leads to no significant conclusion. For in thinking he has in a vital sense already abstracted from his own existence. The existence that is established by thinking (or, more strictly, by doubting) is a thin, logical kind of existence without any real being-in-the-world. Is this a really worthwhile existence? Such a free-floating self might be better than no self at all. But that assumption could, I think, be seriously questioned because insofar as Descartes sets us on the road to nihilism his abstracted self is rather close to a nothing.

There are two consequences of Descartes' method that call for brief mention at this point. One has to do with its ethical irrelevance. When early in life he put forth his "tree" of knowledge, Descartes proposed to unify the main branches of knowledge (mechanics, medicine, physics *and* ethics) in light of certain principles of metaphysics mathematically secured. Consequently, when he begins to reconstruct the philosophical edifice *de novo* he adopts a provisional morality. In the third part of the *Discourse* he explains that "while reason obliged me to be irresolute in my beliefs, there was no reason why I should be so in my actions." He thus agrees to obey "the laws and customs of my country, constantly retaining the religion in which, by God's grace, I had been brought up since childhood, and in all other matters to follow the most moderate and least excessive opinions to be found in the practices of the more judicious part of the community in which I would live." This moral pusillanimity is somewhat surprising in so bold a spirit. Moreover, Descartes never did work out a moral theory. Time, no doubt, was a factor. But it strikes me that as his system emerged he became more and more aware of the irrelevance of ethics. To do ethics in any concrete sense would embroil him in the obscurities of sense knowledge (and thus obfuscate the necessary distinction between mind and body), for ethics is what regulates our being-in-the-world, our action and interpersonal relationships. His method condemned him to maintain the original dualism he postulated between knowledge and morality; he remained a "spectator rather than an actor" in the affairs of men.

The skeptic, of course, has no choice but to conform to the status quo. But in Descartes' case there is something worse: ideas shed no light on the problems of living whatsoever. In ethical matters he compared himself, rather aptly, to a lost traveler. "I patterned my behavior on that of travelers, who, finding themselves lost in a forest, must not wander about, now turning this way, now that, and still less should remain in one place, but should go as straight as they can in the direction they first select and not change the direction except for the strongest reasons. By this method, even if the direction was chosen at random, they will presumably arrive at some destination, not perhaps where they would like to be, but at least where they will be better off than in the middle of the forest." That conclusion is at best dubious. For, as anyone who has ever been lost in a forest knows, one simply turns in circles unless one's direction is guided by something more than random choice. There is here a confused grasp of man's ethical being. The sense of lostness Descartes exhibits has in one way or another characterized much ethical discussion since his time.

The second consequence of methodical doubt I want to mention has to do with the role of the will. In the fourth Meditation, where he is treating of the true and the false, Descartes begins with the remark that he knows more things respecting God than he does respecting corporeal things. His most evident and certain conviction is "that God exists, and that my existence depends entirely on him in every moment of my life." How, then, can the problem of error be accounted for? To answer this question Descartes indulges in some reflections on the paradoxical condition of man: "I am in a sense something intermediate between God and nought, i.e. placed in such a manner between the supreme Being and non-being that there is in truth nothing in me that can lead to error insofar as a sovereign Being has formed me; but that, as I in some degree participate likewise in nought or in non-being, i.e. insofar as I am not myself the supreme Being, and as I find myself subject to an infinitude of imperfections, I ought not be astonished if I should fall into error."

God is thus cleared of any complicity in error. But Descartes has not yet located its precise source. As he continues to ponder the matter he is struck by the disparity between his will and all of his other faculties. The latter are all limited; but the will is subject to no limits. "It is free-will alone or liberty which I find to be so great in me that I can conceive no other idea to be more great." It is this power which makes Descartes aware that he bears "the image and similitude of God," that he is in some sense infinite. But this power of will is not of itself the source of error. Rather the latter is to be found in the fact that, since the will "is much wider in its range and compass than the understanding," it extends to things that are not controlled by the latter and "easily falls into error and sin." This is a strange explanation, predicated upon an intriguing duality and justified by even more intriguing claims. And it is one that links Descartes with a long tradition. Free will had often been called upon to exculpate God and lay the blame for sin and error on man. With Descartes and the Renaissance humanists, emphasis on the autonomous will becomes more explicit and shifts to the center of philosophical speculation. This concept would later find its classical expression in Kant's *Critique of Practical Reason* and be lengthily explored in the various will-to-power tracts of German idealism. And it is, of course, the element of Descartes' philosophy that most appeals to Sartre and other existentialists.

We should not agree that Descartes is guilty of Pascal's harsh judgment: "Useless and uncertain." Or Voltaire's satiric remark to the effect that he disproved the errors of antiquity only to substitute his own (Voltaire himself was rather good at that sort of thing); or a recent poet's condescending "Poor, deceived Frenchman." But he did raise questions that have never been satisfactorily answered: By what right does Cartesian logic enjoin us to pass from the idea of a thing to the thing itself? How do the clarity and distinctness of an idea assure its objective reference? How can we be certain that the real world conforms to the demands of our reason? How, in fact, can we be sure that there is any real world at all? Descartes' genius was to have understood and given brilliant expression to the spirit and intellectual trends of his age. By elaborating a bifurcated vision of reality he thought he had solved the principal problems of his time. We now see that he merely perpetuated them, thus sanctioning the separation of man from his world and exacerbating the problem of self-identity.

John Locke and Man's Lost World

Historians sometimes speak of the "breakdown of Cartesianism" as though it were a system that thrived temporarily only to be supplanted by another. A frequent contrast is Cartesian idealism (or mathematicism) and British empiricism (with its emphasis on experience). If we compare Locke and Descartes the differences between the two thinkers strike us immediately. Locke not only criticized

Descartes on a number of specific points (innate ideas, substances, etc.) but disagreed with his whole approach. He thought that Descartes had radically mistaken the human mind's ability. Whence his resolve to examine our abilities and see "what objects our understandings were or were not fitted to deal with." His prose style exhibits an engaging modesty. The Cartesian ambition has disappeared. Locke is not interested in far-flung metaphysics; he has no yearning to solve all the problems; nor does he thirst after a certainty that would withstand every conceivable objection. Descartes soared to the infinite; Locke was content to remain earth-bound. He merely sought to clear some of the rubbish that clutters the path of knowledge. The universe of discourse, he insisted, must be a limited one. Thus Locke declined "to let loose his thoughts into the vast ocean of being" and determined instead to inquire into "the origin, certainty, and extent of human knowledge." The differences are vast. Still, when we scrutinize the two philosophers more closely we discover an impressive continuity of methodology as well as a similarity in problems raised.

The pertinent tenets of Locke's philosophy, so far as his contribution to the advent of alienation is concerned, may be summarized as follows: (1) All ideas derive from experience (comprising reflection and sensation); (2) Science is a deductive system of mathematically demonstrated connections between material particles; (3) Knowledge consists in the perception of "agreement and disagreement of ideas"; (4) Ideas are in the mind (in much the same way that furniture is in a room); (5) Ideas are objects of understanding, they are the materials of knowledge—knowledge issues from the logical relations between them; (6) Ideas are also "knowledge of objects" and there is real knowledge when there is conformity between our ideas and things.

Locke would have eliminated many avenues to alienation

had he clarified the relationship between the two last men-
tioned points—had he, in other words, resolved more satisfactorily the duality of knower and known, mind and
external world. But by setting forth ideas as mental and
natural objects as physical, and holding that all knowledge of the latter is by means of the former, he raised this
problem: How can mental ideas represent objects that are
radically different from themselves? The obvious source of
Locke's dilemma seems to be the insertion of his conception
of knowledge into the traditional framework of substance.[9]
He is primarily wedded to the notion that the mind has no
other immediate object but its own ideas. Thus it is evident
that "our knowledge is only conversant about them"
(*Essay*, IV, i, 1). The "mind does not know things immediately but only by the intervention of the ideas it has of
them" (*Essay*, IV, iv, 3). Professor Aaron explains Locke's
difficulty in these words: "The immediate object when I
look at this table is no physical entity but an idea which
represents the table. I know physical entities and their
qualities through the mediation of ideas and through ideas
alone . . . The mind does not see the real physical object.
It sees an object which somehow exists in the mind, and yet
is not the mind itself, nor a modification of the mind."[10]

The problem here has a distinct Cartesian flavor: How
do we know the world, or even that there is a world? Locke
is aware of the difficulty. Thus he wonders: "Our knowledge
therefore is real only insofar as there is a conformity between
our ideas and the reality of things. But what shall be here
the criterion? How shall the mind, when it perceives nothing
but its own ideas, know that they agree with things themselves? This seems not to want difficulty" (*Essay*, IV, iv, 3).
The existence of anything beyond sense-data remains shad-
owy. For what criterion could be used to establish the conformity between things and ideas? Locke appeals to the fact

of the mind's passivity in sensation and assumes that there is something "out there" that impresses (causes) such ideas in us. But he is vague as to what that something might be. And, in any event, "having the idea of anything in our mind no more proves the existence of that thing than the picture of a man evidences his being in the world or the visions of a dream make thereby a true history" (*Essay,* IV, xi, 1). Since truth is "nothing but the joining or separating of signs" in terms of their agreement or disagreement with one another, scientific knowledge cannot be hoped for (cf. *Essay,* IV, iii, 26) and the extent of our knowledge is perforce limited (*Essay,* IV, iii, 6). Locke realized that his position was vulnerable, that an objector might well ask: Is this more than building castles in the air? What is the difference between knowledge and dreams? (Compare *Essay,* IV, iv, 1 ff.)

The Cartesian dream syndrome is still with us, and Berkeley's idealism as well as Hume's skepticism lurk just around the corner. Nor does the distinction between primary and secondary qualities really resolve this difficulty. Locke held that the ideas of primary qualities are exact representations of those qualities, while those of secondary qualities are not. But the doctrine of primary qualities cannot safeguard Locke's empiricism until it be shown how we know that the ideas of primary qualities do as a matter of fact resemble the qualities themselves. Curiously enough, Locke nowhere offers proof of this. His discussion bears almost exclusively on secondary qualities. And in no case does he abandon his mentalistic bias. Our knowledge of primary qualities is still knowledge of ideas. And since the status of ideas remains ambiguous the dependent theories likewise lack clarity. The safest general statement we can make about Locke's theory of knowledge is the following: we know things (substances) only through their effects (i.e. the ideas they can produce in us), but no necessary connection between effects and causes can be established. Whence Locke is forced to admit that the real essences of things are hidden from us. Locke has been called a half-realist. He seems to have been a half-hearted one as well. The tentative tone of his argumentation is far from conclusive. "The extent of our knowledge comes not only short of the reality of things, but even of the extent of our own ideas" (*Essay,* IV, iii, 6). The various doubts we have about our ideas, Locke says, are not likely to ever be resolved in this world. We do not know wherein thinking consists, and this state is apparently as the Creator has decreed. In a word, scientific knowledge is out of our reach (cf. *Essay*, IV, iii, 26). Locke takes his final stand in this answer to a putative skeptic:

> For, our faculties being suited not to the full extent of being, nor to a perfect, clear, comprehensive knowledge of things free from all doubt and scruple, but to the preservation of us, in whom they are, and accommodated to the use of life, they serve to our purpose well enough, if they will but give us certain notice of those things which are convenient or inconvenient to us . . . So that this evidence is as great as we can desire, being as certain to us as our pleasure or pain, i.e. happiness or misery; beyond which we have no concernment either of knowing or being [*Essay*, IV, xi, 8].

This seems little more than pyrrhic resignation before the irrational. The existence of the external world is equivalent to supposing that it exists. As Randall says in criticism of Locke: "We know the world only by experience, not by reasoning; yet what we know is not the world, but only experience. We must defer to facts, but there are no facts, only ideas."[11] The root of Locke's dilemma is also a form of reductionism. Intelligibility is not a feature of the world; ideas have a reduced ontological source in things; knowledge ends with the contents of our mind. Thus ideas can be certain but their reality remains questionable. Since things are not what they seem, appearances are forever cloaking reality. On this view the chances for assured knowledge of the extramental are slim. Consequently, a unified vision of the world, which is one of the conditions of dealienation, is precluded. In Dewey's words: "Philosophy will become *modern* in the pregnant sense only when the 'objectivism-subjectivism' involved is seen to be one of cooperative interaction of two distinguishable sets of conditions, so that knowledge of them *in their distinction* is required in order that their interaction may be brought under intentional guidance. Without such knowledge, intelligence is inevitably held down to techniques of making mechanical permutations and combinations of things that *have* been experienced, and mankind is dependent upon accident for the introduction of novelty."[12] This paradox has been the hallmark of empirical philosophy through Hume and Berkeley to Ayer and Russell.*

* Louis Kampf, among others, has called attention to the influence of empiricist psychology on contemporary literary genres such as the literature of the absurd and the *nouveau roman*. The assumption here, he notes, is that the mind cannot make meaningful connections or order the elements of experience in any significant way. "The commitment of eighteenth century men of letters to empiricism," he writes, "allowed literature a salutary sense of freedom, thus making large areas of experience, hardly touched on previously, accessible to all the arts. Yet in our time the literary consequences of empiricism have been corrosive. The notion of art as an experimental report of experience, combined with the unfounded assumption that we attain knowledge in an unstructured way, must eventually lead to chaos." On the other hand, the Romantic desire to impose the mind's order on reality (which stems from the inwardness implied by skeptical doubt) can lead to the arbitrary imposition of formal constructs on experience. Either way there are difficulties in unifying the mental and extra-mental realms. (See Louis Kampf, *On Modernism*, Cambridge, The M.I.T. Press, 1967, pp. 281 ff.)

The Private Self

Locke's treatment of the problem of self-identity is another important antecedent of the contemporary problem of alienation.* Descartes was concerned with this problem (and a good deal of modern-day *angst* can be read into him), but when his system assumed final form, the indivisibility of the self as a thinking substance was a self-evident truth (Meditation VI), and the problem of personal identity was stilled. But Locke did not admit that the mind was furnished with any clear and distinct ideas of substance and therefore could have no intuitive knowledge of its nature. As Henry Allison writes: "Thus, far from affirming with Descartes, that the human understanding possesses an intuitive knowledge of the indivisibility of the soul, Locke even denies that we can have certain knowledge of its immortality, and it is precisely this skepticism in regard to the nature of the soul which posed for Locke the problem of personal identity. For if we do not know that the soul is indivisible, how do we know that it persists through time? And if it does not persist, in what sense can we talk about the person remaining the same?"[13] Still, it was important for Locke to salvage the concept of personal identity for ethical and religious reasons. Consequently, he had to begin by making a sharp distinction between personal identity and substance. For if we were to talk of the former in terms of

---

*Less than fifty years later Hume could say that the problem had become "a great question" in philosophy. From this time onward, William Levi writes, "psychology and, sometimes preceding it and sometimes in its wake, philosophy have been wrestling with the problem of the fragmented self. An epistemological problem with Hume, a social and psychological one with Mead and Freud, it has mostly been the product of some preoccupation with the self as a minded organism and a center of decision."
—"On Being Oneself," *Ethics,* Vol. LXV (1965–66), p. 307.

the latter we would be unable to determine clearly the domain of moral responsibility.[14]

Locke defines human identity as "a participation of the same continued life, by constantly fleeting particles of matter, in succession vitally united to the same organized body" (*Essay* II, xxvii, 6). The emphasis has already shifted from the Cartesian substance, and identity now implies a determinate size and shape. "For if identity of soul alone makes the same man, and there be nothing in the nature of matter why the same individual spirit may not be united to different bodies, it will be possible that those men living in distant ages, and of different tempers, may have been the same man" (*Essay* II, xxvii, 6). This idea of man is but a first step. Locke still hasn't answered the question of *personal* identity. He consequently inquires into the nature of person and defines it as "a thinking intelligent being, that has reason and reflection, and can consider itself as itself, the same thinking thing, in different times and places; which it does only by that consciousness which is inseparable from thinking, and it seems to me essential to it." (*Essay* II, xxvii, 9) The conclusion is now obvious: consciousness makes personal identity. In an important passage he says:

> For since consciousness always accompanies thinking, and it is that that makes everyone to be what he calls self, and thereby distinguishes himself from all other thinking things; in this alone consists personal identity, i.e. the sameness of the rational being; and as far as this consciousness can be extended backwards to any past action or thought, so far reaches the identity of that person; it is the same self now as it was then; and it is by the same self with this present one that now

reflects on it, that that action was done [*Essay*, II, xxvii, 9].

Two remarks may be made here. First, it must be noted that Locke has adopted a Cartesian conception of consciousness as necessarily involving self-consciousness. But since he has rejected the Cartesian substance that supports this view, he is forced to make self-consciousness co-extensive with remembered states. His distinction between personal and substantial identity burdens the memory with the whole weight of moral responsibility. Locke then proceeds to deal with some obvious objections. Has the same person performed unremembered acts? What about a somnambulist or a drunkard? His answers here are rather forced and unconvincing. At the end of the chapter, person is reduced to "a forensic term, appropriating actions and their merit; and so belongs only to intelligent agents, capable of law, and happiness and misery" (*Essay*, II, xxvii, 26). This admission necessitates some modification of Locke's original position. Since he never worked this out, his solution has remained extremely annoying. As Allison assesses his effort:

> Thus considered, the notion of "person" enables Locke to provide a clear and decisive basis for moral responsibility. However, it also raises the serious question . . . that perhaps this consistency was bought at the price of relevance. By abstracting one aspect from the concrete man, and calling that the "person," he can account for personal identity and moral responsibility; but in gaining this too easy victory, he may have ignored the more serious problem of the identity and responsibility of man.[15]

Locke admitted, with characteristic modesty, that some of his affirmations will look strange to some readers "and possibly are so in themselves." But he excuses himself on the grounds of our general ignorance about reality and especially "the thinking thing that is in us." It may be admitted that Locke's intentions were praiseworthy. It may be counted a step forward to have separated the concept of identity (or unity of consciousness) from the ghosty doctrine of the identity of an immaterial substance. That he did not resolve it must not be considered too surprising in light of the fact that it has not been resolved even today. Locke raised for contemporary philosophy what was to become a distinct and very lively issue.

Some of the consequences of this issue have been examined by Alfred Duhrssen.[16] Discussing the problem of alienation and other minds, he effects a curious blend of empirical language and existential phantasmagoria. The gestures of our fellow men, he says, are sometimes opaque and grotesque. The world becomes Kafkaesque: voices are heard but not understood; clocks tick meaninglessly; bodies meet and touch only to dissolve before the eyes unite in love. Such a situation leads to the philosophical, and very Lockean, question of how I can know that I am not alone in the world, a voice in the desert. "For the philosophically alienated personality, at once abstracted and distracted, mind is an inner activity of perception, a ceaseless stream of thoughts, feelings, and volitions, revealed to the one who withdraws into himself but concealed from him who gazes merely at the world before him."[17] How can we know another's thoughts? How does communication take place? Obviously we have to engage in some kind of bridge-building. We reconstruct after the fact. We perceive outward signs in the other's behavior; this by analogy reminds me of my own behavior and my own mental activity. It therefore becomes a matter of predicating of the other what is the case with me. But this effort is vitiated by serious doubt. Descartes returns to tell us that we really can't see anything. "And that which I thought I saw with my eyes, I understood by the sole faculty of judging which is my mind" (Meditation II). All wax melts; hats and coats may cover scarecrows.

The argument from analogy seems to break down. Some philosophers who take this problem seriously have suggested a method of logical construction. This leads to substituting logical fictions for things and considering the other person as the "logical class of his experiences" (Russell). Knowledge of other minds would then consist in constructing the other's body from private sense data and then further constructing a mind for that body. But, queries Duhrssen, "How can I lump together, or collect in a bundle, sense data which, if they are mine, are evanescent and which, if they are another's, are invisible, impalpable, and so forth? There are absolutely no operations which correspond to the formation of a physical object in the sense of a logical construct from sense data."[18] This would appear to be a reasonable objection. Traditional rationalism and empiricism have never overcome the dualism of body and soul. The difficulty is built into the very vocabulary of that tradition.

If alienation, in one of its important meanings, is not to be at home in the world, then we might ask why we are alienated. The answer would seem to be that our home is elsewhere. Inquiry reveals that we dwell in the privacy of our flow of sense data. But this is not a happy abode. The only way we can know another, Duhrssen suggests, is to put ourselves in "his place." But this kind of transference is fraught with difficulties. Speech seems to afford the best means of doing this. The self exists in some privileged way in vocal utterances. Thus we can know one another in the shared universe of discourse. But this insight is as old as recorded history. Today many consider it naïve, for it has been abundantly impressed upon us of late that language itself has been victimized by alienation. Is death the only answer?

We can scarcely imagine Locke accepting that judgment. But we have seen how his epistemological principles and handling of the problem of personal identity bear on the problem of alienation. The conception of the Cogito as the foremost characteristic of rationality is what profoundly unites Locke and Descartes. Leibnitz, although he was critical of Locke, also holds to this view, which reaches its logical destiny in Kant's distinction between the noumenal and phenomenal selves and the transcendental unity of apperception. At this point the "I think" has become a purely formal principle (that which accompanies all other representations), a mere abstraction.

---

1. Fernando Molina, *Existentialism as Philosophy* (Englewood Cliffs, Prentice-Hall, 1962), p. 33.
2. See his article "Husserl's Critique of Descartes," *Philosophy and Phenomenological Research*, Vol. XXIII (1962–63), p. 338.
3. Erwin Straus, "Anesthesiology and Hallucinations," in *Existence: A New Dimension in Psychiatry and Psychology*, edited by Rollo May, Ernest Angel and Henri F. Ellenberger (New York, Basic Books, 1958), pp. 139–170.
4. A. N. Whitehead, *Science and the Modern World* (New York, Mentor, 1950), p. 12.
5. Fernando Molina, *op. cit.*, p. 36.
6. Alexandre Koyré, "Introduction," in *Descartes: Philosophical Writings*, edited by Elizabeth Anscombe and Peter Thomas Geach (London, Thomas Nelson and Sons, 1964), p. xxxii.

7. Richard Popkin, *The History of Skepticism from Erasmus to Descartes* (Assen, Netherlands, Van Gorcum & Co., 1960), p. 190.

8. Karsten Harries, "Irrationalism and Cartesian Method," *Journal of Existentialism*, Vol. VII (1960), p. 295.

9. See John Dewey, "Substance, Power and Quality in Locke," in *Freedom and Experience*, edited by Sidney Hook (Ithaca, Cornell University Press, 1947), pp. 204–220. Dewey notes further: "In the final analysis opposition between the inner constitution and essence (which Locke retained from prior metaphysics) and the relations which are knowable (his own contribution) is the source of the opposition which we are familiar with as the Lockean contrast between idea and object" (p. 206).

10. Richard Aaron, *John Locke* (London, Oxford, 1955), p. 106.

11. John Herman Randall, Jr., *The Career of Philosophy*, p. 301.

12. John Dewey, *Problems of Men* (New York, The Philosophical Library, 1946), p. 321.

13. Henry Allison, "Locke's Theory of Personal Identity: a Re-Examination," *The Journal of the History of Ideas*, Vol. XXVII (1966), p. 41.

14. Few doctrines have been so soundly criticized. For a typical indictment see A. Flew, "Locke and the Problem of Personal Identity," *Philosophy*, Vol. XXVI (1951), pp. 53–68.

15. Allison, *op. cit.*, p. 48.

16. Alfred Duhrssen, "Philosophic Alienation and the Problem of Other Minds," *The Philosophical Review*, Vol. LXIX (1960), pp. 211–220.

17. *Ibid.*, p. 211.

18. *Ibid.*, p. 215.

The Quest for

Wholeness

The rationalist tradition may be looked upon as a powerful tributary flowing into the Kantian synthesis. It was only temporarily halted there, however. When it became apparent that Kant had not resolved the problems raised by his predecessors but only systematized their assumptions, they emerged anew in the German idealism of the late eighteenth and early nineteenth centuries. By this time another important current was swelling the intellectual waters. Among the ways in which rationalism furnished important antecedents for what is now known as the problem of alienation was its failure to integrate man into his social milieu. Auguste Cornu states the matter in these words: "Rationalism is led to conceive of man as an individual opposed to his social milieu and cannot therefore arrive at a conception of the world as an organic whole; it remains essentially dualistic and allows the traditional opposition to subsist between spirit and matter, man and nature."[1] Such thinkers as Grotius, Hobbes, Locke, Spinoza and the French encyclopedists belied a concern with the social aspects of alienation in their various treatises on government, inalienable rights and social contracts. In one way or another they asked: Why is man estranged from his reason so that he lives irrationally? And what must be done to correct this state of affairs? The problematic status of man in bourgeois society had early come to the attention of the intelligentsia. Eighteenth-century thinkers became aware that the problem was a major one.

Vico, for example, made his central concern the nature of man in human society. Against the disciples of Descartes, the mathematicians and natural scientists who dominated the intellectual scene of his day, Vico took the unpopular stand that the abstract method of the formal disciplines imparts no real knowledge about the world. We cannot understand the external world in any depth, he argued, because we did not create it. Man can truly understand only what he himself created. This includes, of course, such disciplines as mathematics and logic. But these are of limited value for understanding reality because of their abstract nature. Vico proposed a historical method for man's self-understanding: to investigate the cultural expressions of the past is to come to know what man himself has created. These provide a means of interhuman communication that enable us to understand man from *within*. Vico thus rejected the Renaissance stress on "perspectivity." Language, art, myth, law and religion—these translate man's historical efforts to build his world and communicate directly to us in terms of human meanings. History rather than scientific method was for Vico the touchstone of self-understanding, without which all other knowledge is meaningless.[2]

The Inauthentic Condition of Man

Rousseau reasoned in a not unsimilar vein. His principal concern was also the unity of man, and he was keenly aware that man in his time was not unified. Karl Löwith observes that Rousseau's writings "contain the first and clearest statement of the human problem in bourgeois society."[3] In the opening chapter of *Emile*, Rousseau writes: "He who would preserve the supremacy of natural feelings in social life knows not what he asks. Ever at war with himself, hesitating between his wishes and his duties, he will be neither a man or a citizen; he will be of no use to himself or others. He will be a man of our day, a Frenchman, an Englishman, one of the great middle class." In his eyes the modern bourgeois was neither a citizen as he had been in the ancient polis, nor a whole man as he was in the state of nature. He was a divided creature. Hans Barth claims Rousseau as the first thinker "in whom the constitutive elements of self-estrangement appear."[4] In light of my foregoing analysis I would not be prepared to accept Barth's assessment literally. But it is true that with Rousseau the problem of alienation comes more explicitly to the forefront of intellectual concern, and its societal dimensions are more extensively explored. He anticipated Kant, Hegel and Marx in some rather remarkable respects, and the modern tonality of his diagnosis is unmistakable. There is much truth to the suggestion that he is the first of our radical thinkers. He was, at any rate, the first major thinker to concentrate on the alienated condition of man as the outcome of economic interests. In exploring the history of inequality Rousseau found that "the establishment of law and of the right of property was the first stage, the institution of the magistracy the second, and the third and last was the changing of legitimate power into arbitrary power. So that the status of the rich and poor was authorized by the first epoch, that of powerful and weak by the second, and by the third that of master and slave . . ." Rousseau asked the question that most urgently occupies us today: How is it that society shackles human freedom and thwarts man's fulfillment?

By alienation Rousseau meant in general* the inauthentic condition of man which results from the corrupt and contradictory character of society. Being-appearance, transparency-opacity, autonomy-heteronomy, nature-society, sensibility-reason, the private and public selves—these were some of the main dichotomies he saw that pointed to the pervasiveness of alienation. The contradiction between being and appearance is perhaps his most usual way of formulating the problem. "Everyone seeks his happiness in appearance; all, slaves and dupes of self-love, live not for the sake of living but only to give the impression that they have lived."

It is the reality-appearance conflict which, according to Starobinski, "engenders all other conflicts, like a series of amplified echoes; rupture between good and evil, nature and society, man and his gods, man and himself."[5] In his first *Discourse* (1750), Rousseau stressed the contradiction between the natural and the artificial, the promotion of the latter by the arts and sciences and their consequent implication in the dissolution of society. "There prevails in our morals an abject and deceptive uniformity, and all minds seem to be cast in the same mold. Endlessly politeness makes demands, decorum gives orders; endlessly we follow customs, never our own bent. We no longer dare seem what we are; and, in this perpetual constraint the men who form this herd which we call society will all do the same things under the same circumstances."

Society is an artificial world which militates against human development because it demands certain forms of behavior and imposes uniformity as its chief characteristic.

---

* As opposed to his strict use of the word "alienation" to mean the surrender or transferral of the particular self and its rights to the larger community. Rousseau viewed this sense of alienation in a very positive light since the social gain was expected to outweigh by far the individual's loss. Compare pages 134 ff.

As such, society requires the sacrifice of original individuality and idealism; it forbids genuine self-expression and effective action; it fosters hypocrisy and falsehood and lends to "total deprivation." Mario Einaudi interprets Rousseau's view of society as "a forced cohabitation of men of conflicting interests who are moved only by a latent desire to destroy one another at the first opportunity. In the society of man brought to flower in the seventeenth and eighteenth centuries, everything is reduced to property and competition. The mask of mutual benevolence hides an ever-present urge to destroy those who may stand in the way of the further acquisition of personal advantages. The multiplication of private needs does not lead to an increase of public benefits, as the economists of the time were saying, but rather to the multiplication of wounds inflicted on private men, to a rise in the tensions of society, to a weakening of the chances of people and happiness."[6] Culture and reality are antipodal and when man conforms his life to such artificial and anonymous models he ceases to be himself and lives a life that is primarily determined from without. Not only have the arts and sciences not been beneficial to man; they have made a major contribution to creating the empty social façade. Cultural refinement and moral degeneration are synonymous terms. Rousseau's position is that the arts and sciences are tainted in their origin (deriving from such undesirable human characteristics as ambition, hatred, vanity and deceit) and are, in their present state, associated with dubious objectives. Thus he explains that the arts are one with luxury, law is born of injustice and history deals almost exclusively with tyranny and war. On the whole, the arts and sciences are born of idleness, and indulgence in them is a waste of time that ought to be profitably spent doing good. Rousseau has special words of condemnation for the pursuit of wealth because it displaces the basis of human worth from moral to economic values. He is not arguing that there is a basic contradiction between knowledge and virtue. Nor is he maintaining that the arts and sciences are intrinsically evil. Rather, he is concerned with denouncing their corruptive influence, their *misuses*.

It cannot be said that he made his point either very clearly or very accurately in this first *Discourse*. It is fraught with the wildest of generalizations. Small wonder it provoked some seventy denunciations, including a vindictive rebuttal by Voltaire. Still, it contains many insights which become important as well as more comprehensible in light of his later writings. Above all, it reveals Rousseau's awareness of the contradictions in life and adumbrates a fundamental equation between morality and politics: to wit, men are unhappy because society has diverted them from their real interests and set them in contradiction with themselves. In Broome's words: "What is already taking shape here is the doctrine that, in turning from nature, the so-called civilized man has burdened himself with the necessity of living a lie, or a series of lies; and that life has become a competition in pursuit of spurious values. Most of the constructive thought of his later works will be concerned in one way or another with the resolution of this conflict between *être* and *paraître,* and the search for authentic values which alone can restore to man his happiness and peace of mind."[7]

Rousseau's second *Discourse* (1755) was an extension and clarification of this doctrine. The most important (and controversial) feature of the *Discourse on Inequality* is the historical hypothesis of natural man. A good deal of the controversy associated with this hypothesis can be avoided if we bear in mind that Rousseau is not describing the state of nature that actually existed. He makes his intention in

this essay clear enough: "For it is by no means a light under-
taking to distinguish properly between what is original and
what is artificial in the actual nature of man, or to form a
true idea of a state which no longer exists, perhaps never
did exist, and probably never will exist; and of which it is,
nevertheless, necessary to have true ideas, in order to form
a proper judgment of our present state." Natural man is not
a historical figure but something more like a theoretical
construct in light of which one can elaborate suitable human
ideals and pronounce judgment upon the social fiction. Rousseau was not urging a return to some imagined state. He was
holding up an ideal model, something for man to strive for.
His thinking was futuristic. Thus when he speaks of natural
man (in contrast to social or conventional man), he wants us
to understand him as referring to ideal man, what truly
civilized man could be. Alienation can be overcome, Rousseau is saying, only by transforming the artificial and unjust
laws that enslave men into the natural laws of reason. His
abiding conviction was not only that man is good and
rational in his natural (ideal) state but that he can become
so actually. This does not imply the destruction of culture
but its transformation. The historical process is irreversible.
But it is convertible and perfectible. Rousseau thought in
terms of reform rather than reincarnation, progress rather
than regress. Man did not have to submit to his alienated
condition.

In a preface to a slight drama he had written in 1752
(*Narcisse*) the revolutionary tone was already apparent.
There Rousseau announced the news that all social evils
were the result of bad government. "*Tous ces vices n'appar-
tiennent pas tant à l'homme qu' à l'homme mal gouverné.*"
Thus: "It is not a question of emancipating and liberating
the individual in the sense of releasing him from the form

and order of the community; it is, rather, a question of find-ing the kind of community that will protect every individual with the whole concerted power of the political organization, so that the individual in uniting himself with all others never-theless obeys only himself in this act of union."[8] Rousseau's hypothetical primitive, although amoral and apolitical, was created by a good God and was himself good. The principal cause of his "fall" was selfish interest (*amour propre*) which leads, through successive social revolutions, to our present sorry state. Pride, especially as expressed in the greedy acquisition of property is, in one way or another, responsi-ble for this state. Rousseau says that the first man to appro-priate property was the real founder of civil society and adds: "From how many crimes, wars, and murders, from how many horrors and misfortunes might not anyone have saved mankind, by pulling up the stakes, or filling up the ditch, and crying to his fellows: 'Beware of listening to this impostor; you are undone if you once forget that the fruits of the earth belong to us all, and the earth itself to nobody.' "

The moral outcome of the despotic nature of property and the corruptive influence of the arts and science is that man has become enslaved to artificial needs. Thus, by con-trasting the state of nature with the state of nature (the ideal-real dialectic) Rousseau is able to give a sharp edge to his social critique. There is such a disparity between natural man and social man that what constitutes the happi-ness of one would plunge the other into darkest despair. Social man—who is "always active, sweats, agitates him-self, torments himself incessantly in order to seek still more laborious occupations"—is quite simply bad. Most of his ills could have been avoided by "preserving the simple, uniform, and solitary way of life prescribed to us by nature." Being and appearing have become two altogether different things. In natural man the two coincided. He was in agreement with himself. Social man has lost this concinnity; he is divided between what he is and what he seems to be. This fragmentation is the cause of his unhappiness. "Natural man lives in himself; social man is outside of himself and can only live in the opinion of others. He draws an awareness of his own existence from their judgment." Thus we must ask others who we are. "Honor without virtue, reason without wisdom, enjoyment without happiness." Rousseau encapsulates his reading of the human condition in that formula. In other words, social man has lost his autonomy and accepted the extraneous norms of society as regulative of his life. And society treats the individual as a limb, an adjunct, and thus leaves him only a relative existence. Social man is denied the unity and integrity of his natural state, and robbed of the ability and right to be whole. Starobinski offers a probant summary of Rousseau's thinking in the first two *Discourses*:

> Man alienates himself in appearances . . . An abstract category that causes all kinds of concrete evils, appearance explains both the interior division of social man, his slavery and the unlimited character of his needs. He is at the antipodes of the happiness which primitive man knew in abandoning himself to the immediate. For the man of appearance there are only means and man himself is reduced to a means. None of his desires can be immediately satisfied; he must pass through the imaginary and the factitious; the opinion of others and the labor of others are indispensable to him. Since men no longer seek to satisfy their "real needs" but only those created by vanity, they are

constantly outside of themselves, strangers to themselves, slaves to one another. When Rousseau denounces social alienation he clearly prefigures Kant and Hegel all in retaining the language of a Stoic moralist.[9]

On the Overcoming of Alienation

How is man to become dealienated? Or, what comes to the same thing, how can the ideal fulfillment of man be brought about? The question is a profoundly moral one and therefore, in Rousseau's thinking, necessarily political. The question in the end becomes: What ideal societal arrangement can be constructed to cancel out alienation? It was one of Rousseau's abiding convictions that man must be educated to the political order; he must become a man before he can be a citizen; or, better, only on condition that he is fully humanized can he function as a citizen. The following passage from *Emile* makes the point: "In the natural order men are all equal and their common calling is that of manhood, so that well-educated man cannot fail to do well in that calling and those related to it. It matters little to me whether my pupil is intended for the army, the church, or the law. Before his parents choose a calling for him nature called him to be a man. Life is the trade I would teach him. When he leaves me, I grant you . . . he will be a man."

This tract is characterized by a double emphasis: the promotion of freedom and attentiveness to the natural rhythm of development. In Book I, Rousseau considers the stage of infancy. The important thing here is to satisfy the child's genuine physical needs such as food (mother's milk), fresh air, hygiene, freedom of movement (no restrictive clothing) and the need for communication (e.g. crying). Nature has equipped the infant with adequate means of expressing its needs; the duty of the educator at this level is to see to it that they are satisfied. Book II treats what Rousseau calls the Age of Sensations and extends to roughly the ages four to twelve. This is a period of emergent moral personhood, and the first lessons of freedom must be instilled during this time, lessons (we might point out) that will serve the future Emile in good stead as a citizen. Rousseau makes a fundamental distinction at this juncture. We can be dependent upon things (i.e. circumstances which are decreed by nature) or upon men (the artificial conventions of society and the opinion of others). The first kind of dependence is in perfect conformity with freedom and morality. The second is not. It is rather the source of all immorality. And in words that bear directly upon the political analysis of *The Social Contract,* Rousseau writes: "If there is any cure for the evil of society, it is to be found in the substitution of law for the individual; in arming the general will with a real strength, beyond the power of any individual will. If the laws of nations, like the laws of nature, could never be broken by any human power, dependence on men would become dependence on things, all the advantages of a state of nature would be combined with all the advantages of social life in the commonwealth. The liberty which preserves a man from vice would be united with the morality that raises him to virtue."

Rousseau's educational program at this stage is to "follow the order of nature by teaching the child dependence on things." Thus the emphasis should be on the education of the senses. Consequently, abstract book learning is ruled out. The child's mind should remain idle as long as possible. Emile should, like Robinson Crusoe, test himself against the requirements of nature through physical experience. Restrictive discipline is necessary during this period. Combined with the lessons of nature it will teach Emile how to suffer. This is important because human happiness is proportionate to knowing and accepting the conditions of life. Some critics have criticized Rousseau on this score. They allege that he wanted to make a primitive savage out of Emile. But this is to ignore the continuity of his thinking and fail to appreciate the implicit theory of knowledge in his educational ideas. Rousseau did not flout rational powers or maintain that children are deprived of them. Obeying the dictates of what he took to be nature's rhythm, he claimed that the child does not exercise its reason abstractly but sensually and imaginatively. The role of the mentor assumes greater importance now. To help Emile make the transition to abstract thinking calls for great skill and delicacy. Book learning should still be secondary. It is primarily important to teach a trade (such as carpentry) and introduce the pupil to the elementary issues of mathematics and economics. Thus the intellect is gradually awakened, and Emile begins to appreciate natural values and prepares himself to judge rightly between the legitimate claims of self-interest and the spurious values of selfish interest that he will encounter in society. He must also at this time come to some understanding of the mutual dependence of men, a point of capital importance with respect to the social contract. Rousseau's aim is to produce *un être agissant et pensant* who at the end of childhood will be conditioned to accept the yoke of necessity imposed by nature and prepared to enter into creative relations with other men by practicing the social virtues.

Adolescence is a critical phase. Rousseau coins the images of a storm and a sleepwalker on the edge of a precipice to accentuate the omnipresent dangers of selfish interest at this time. The two principal dangers are associated with the newly awakened sexual desire and the beginning of genuine intellectual curiosity. The first, always under the guidance of the mentor, will be resolved in family life, and the second by a sound education in abstract speculation (metaphysics, languages and literature, religion and social theory). Thus is formed the family man and the citizen. Book V makes it clear that the purpose of *Emile* is to outline a preparatory program for civil responsibility. Here Rousseau stresses the unity of his political thought and the moral and natural virtues of his pupil. He also points out the interaction of family and social life; a happy blend of rational activity and emotional fulfillment favors the realization of a genuine society. As we have indicated, such a society for Rousseau is one in which the ideal potential of man can be realized and alienation canceled out.

A passage in *The Confessions* indicates how Rousseau formulated the question of political theory:

> I had seen that everything is rooted in politics and that, whatever might be attempted, no people would ever be other than the nature of their government made them. So the great question of the best possible government seemed to me to reduce itself to this: "What is the nature of the government best fitted to create the most virtuous, the most enlightened, the wisest, and, in fact, the best people, taking the word 'best' in its highest sense?" I believed that I saw a close relationship between

that question and another, very nearly though not quite the same: "What is the government which by its nature always adheres closest to the law?" From which one comes to: "What is the law?" and to a chain of questions of that magnitude.

The touchstone of the political order as Rousseau conceived it was the following: all rights and responsibilities for both rulers and citizens are derived from some agreement, a contract. This contract in fact creates society and delivers man from the amoral, apolitical, unreflective immediacy of the state of nature. As a result of the contract, rational behavior replaces instinct, a moral sense of responsibility replaces physical motivation, and law replaces appetite. From "a stupid and dull-witted animal" there evolves "an intelligent being and man." It is important to note that man is for Rousseau an essentially social creature. Here he differs from such political theorists as Hobbes, Locke and others whose philosophy assumed a more egotistical conception of man. For them social institutions exercise a negative function of protecting rights and controlling excessive individualism. Rousseau demands more. Social institutions of their very nature must promote human fulfillment. Here Rousseau seems to imply that wrongly conceived individualism is a source of alienation, more or less synonymous with selfish interest. In this case, society could be no more than a collection of individuals with conflicting, indeed contradictory, goals and wills. By insisting that through the contract man becomes a social creature with a social conscience, concerned for the welfare of all, the total *bien-être* of society, Rousseau was in fact reintroducing a classical, participative ideal of man in society.

The Joining of Wills

But how can such an ideal be realized, human nature being what it is? It is a question of finding "a form of association which defends and protects with a common force the person and the welfare of each associate and by means of which each one by uniting with all nonetheless only obeys himself and remains just as free as he was before." The social contract demands "the total alienation of each associate with all his rights to the whole community." Rousseau urges a secular version of the biblical losing the whole world in order to gain one's soul. As a result of the joining of wills by the social contract a general will, not to be confused with the will of all (or collection of individual wills), comes into being. "Each man by giving himself to all, gives himself to nobody; and since there is no associate over whom he does not acquire the same right that he has given the other over himself, he gains the equivalent of everything he has lost and more power to preserve what he has." The general will is the will of the body politic, exercised through democratic assemblies. Furthermore, since sovereignty is the expression of the general will and the general will is the expression of the will of all, sovereignty cannot be alienated by anyone or delegated to anyone—king or elected representative. Against the divine right of kings and all forms of despotism, Rousseau is arguing for a basically democratic regime. His intention was to construct a political system in which heteronomy and autonomy would be harmoniously mediated. Hence the priority of self-legislation over laws imposed from without. In other words, man submits to a law that he has willed himself. Since he has willed it himself it cannot be alien or alienating. Through it man legislates his own existence and lives authentically.

What Rousseau is trying to establish, says Hans Barth, is law and reason in the *corps politique*. He is striving for an association in which self-estrangement would be ruled out. "The object of the general will, one cannot put it any other way, is a mental, rational, moral reality which precedes the unification of the political body and becomes its formal gauge . . . In the general will man affirms the rational and just will as the reason and standard of the political body."[10] Obedience to self-imposed laws is the condition of liberty. Thus individual will, which is subjective and motivated by selfish interest, must be sacrificed to the objective rationale of the general will. Virtue is, in fact, the conformity of the particular will to the general will. Thus the contradiction that is at the heart of all forms of alienation will, hopefully, be ruled out and a rational unity will prevail. Then man will really become himself and exist as a whole. He will then live in terms of his true self and become what he should and can be. The heart of the social question was, for Rousseau, not a matter of releasing the individual from the strictures of law and discipline as many Romantic interpretations would have it. Rather it was a matter of finding the kind of law and discipline that would bring about fulfillment.

This is an important source of Kant's theory of the good will and categorical imperative. Kant, history records, placed Rousseau's thought side by side with Newton's in importance. What Kant appreciated in Rousseau was the clear distinction he made between "the mask that man wears and his actual visage." Rousseau, he felt, discovered the true ethical nature of man, and this rather than physical nature is the essential human element. For both Rousseau and Kant, an autonomous personality and authentic morality is possible only in terms of a universal, objective law which man should derive from himself in accordance with the determination of his own free will. Such a law is universally binding and banishes all trace of caprice and arbitrariness. The law of the community (general will) in this respect parallels the law of nature: the price of freedom is to accept the necessary and make personal appropriation of it. Only on this condition can the perversity of selfish interest be purified and willfulness develop into will. "Law in its pure and strict sense is not a mere external bond that holds in individual wills and prevents their scattering; rather it is the constituent principle of these wills, the element that confirms and justifies them spiritually. It wishes to rule subjects only inasmuch as, in its every act, it also makes and educates them into citizens."[11]

It is in light of Rousseau's political theory and his subordination of politics to an ethical imperative that the fundamental unity of his vision can be understood. He evinces a vision of a unified and rational world conspicuously more complete than, say, that of Descartes, Locke or Hobbes. Because his philosophy was man-centered (rather than mathematical or atomistic) he was able to broaden the concept of reason to include sensibility and feeling. He restored, we might say, the moral dimension to rationalistic thinking and banished all forms of metaphysics that would not account for the totality of man's nature and permit of a coincidence between human and cosmic nature. Truth, for him, involved the whole man fully aware of his situation in society and in the universe. He saw clearly that human life cannot be separated from the larger order of things. To be dealienated means to be at one with, at home in, a whole world that is characterized by goodness and rationality.

Such, at any rate, was Rousseau's vision. Whether his

own philosophy could effect this happy state is another question. As a matter of fact I do not think it could. Although I am not primarily concerned here with a critique of Rousseau, I would like to mention two serious weaknesses in his philosophy. In the first place he retains a good deal of the traditional dualism between spirit and matter. In one of his letters he wrote: "Man is not a simple being; he is composed of two substances . . . Whence self-love cannot be a simple passion. It has two principles, namely the intelligent being and the sensual being. These two principles envisage different goods. The sensual appetite tends towards the goods of the body and love of order tends towards the good of the soul." There is much of Augustine's spirit carried over in Rousseau. This dualistic bias led him to postulate conflicts between man and society that are misleading. The conflict between our natural inclinations and social obligations, for example, need not be as radical as Rousseau held them to be. His social contract is in some sense a secular version of the fall-redemption dialectic and calls for a radical change in the human substance, a literal rebirth. But any effort to secularize the Christian scheme is usually vitiated by similar problems. What is lacking in Rousseau's proposal is a proper sense of relative goods and the limited character of the ends-means continuum.

My second line of criticism centers on Rousseau's hypostatization of the will. Dealienation must be brought about by the quasi-mystical mechanism of the general will. Man must will to be forced to be free. This paradoxical recommendation is as troublesome as any religious fiat. It is logically inconsistent; it cannot be enforced and it is circular (in that it appears to assume the very state it is intended to create). If at the time of the contract there is complete harmony between the will of all and the general will, then the latter also seems superfluous. Rousseau would seem to be postulating a kind of transcendental entity beyond what the situation calls for. This, as has often been charged, opens the door to emotionalism and perverted political mystiques. Camus, for example, makes this criticism and calls attention to the charged emotive language—words like *absolute, sacred, inviolable*—that are frequently used in *The Social Contract.* In the end, Rousseau glorifies the will to the unconditioned. The liberty he prescribes to that extent lacks empirical grounding and is severed from rational control. From this point of view I would argue that Rousseau substituted one form of alienation for another.

His diagnosis was far superior to his proposed solutions and that is why the problem of alienation cannot be adequately discussed without reference to him. He understood that the development of "rationalistic" metaphysic was gradually negating human and ethical significance; its social counterpart (exemplified primarily in bourgeois capitalism) was having the same effect. Such insights and his powerful critique against the prevailing situation are the principal reasons why he speaks so plainly to contemporary man. For our alienation is directly related to that feeling of helplessness caused by the anonymity and constrictive grip of social powers. We realize today that the institutions we have created serve our needs badly, that we have created an opaque and alien world which presses intolerably on the human spirit. Rousseau foresaw many of the causes of our ills: the disintegration of community, our divorce from nature, the separation between ethics and politics, the loneliness of man in the great urban agglomerations. Lionel Grossman writes to the point. "Modern sensibility," he says, "which Rousseau did much to cultivate and explore, develops in growing opposition to society . . . Thus it brings with it not joy and fulfillment but misery and alienation, for it cuts the individual off from others without rebuilding the bridges that lead to them . . . Awakened sensibility demands a new society constructed on its own principles of love and sympathy."[12] But this is an ideal that is unresolvably opposed by the actual structure of society—whether in the eighteenth or twentieth century. Rousseau's analysis of alienation and corruption is the principal inspiration for all later efforts to dealienate man and set the condition, for the realization of human freedom.

1. Auguste Cornu, "Hegel, Marx and Engels," in *Philosophy for the Future*, edited by Roy Wood Sellars, V. J. McGill and Marvin Farber (New York, Macmillan, 1949), p. 42.
2. See A. R. Caponigri, *Time and Idea: The Theory of History in Giambattista Vico* (Chicago, Regnery, 1953).
3. Karl Löwith, *From Hegel to Nietzsche* (New York, Doubleday, 1967), pp. 232 ff.
4. Hans Barth, "Die Idee der Selbstenfremdung bei Rousseau," in *Wahreit und Ideologie* (Zurich, 1961), p. 102.
5. Jean Starobinski, *Jean Jacques Rousseau: La Transparence et l'Obstacle* (Paris, Plon, 1957), p. 2.
6. Mario Einaudi, *The Early Rousseau* (Ithaca, Cornell University Press, 1967), p. 136.
7. J. H. Broome, *Rousseau: A Study of His Thought* (New York, Barnes & Noble, 1963), p. 38.
8. *Ibid.*
9. Starobinski, *op. cit.*, p. 32.
10. Hans Barth, *op. cit.*, p. 119.
11. Ernst Cassirer, *Rousseau, Kant and Goethe* (New York, Harper Torchbooks, 1945), p. 63.
12. Lionel Grossman, "Time and History in Rousseau," in *Studies on Voltaire and the 18th Century*, edited by Theodore Besterman, Vol. XXX (Geneva, 1964), pp. 329–330.

The Highway of

Despair

The category of freedom was to be of special concern to the idealists (especially the Germans) of the nineteenth century and was closely connected with their various proposals for the solution of the problem of alienation, a problem they considered generally in terms of the inauthentic forms of experience. What they tried to do was to bring the self and the alien non-self into some satisfactory rapport. This was a major concern of Fichte, Schelling, Schopenhauer, Schiller, Hölderlin and Goethe among others. Fichte, for example, dwelt extensively on the idea of lost and regained freedom. His primary objective was to free man from the determinisms in the universe that had been served up by the rationalist philosophers. All the idealists held that the human self can somehow escape the causal limitations that characterize the rest of the created order. Thus Fichte's idealism enabled him to view the objective world as posited by man's own creative activity. Consequently, it is the world that is dependent upon man and not the other way around. Schiller, in his *Letters,* considers alienation as a disparity between man's existence "in time" and his authentic nature "in idea." The main business of life is to harmonize the two; otherwise man remains "fragmented" and "dismembered." In a strongly Rousseauian vein he says it was culture that dismembered man through the division of sciences and of labor. Consequently, "enjoyment was separated from labor, means from ends, effort from reward. Eternally chained to only one single little fragment of the whole, man himself grew to be only a fragment; with the monotonous noise of the wheel he drives everlastingly in his ears, he never develops the harmony of his being, and instead of imprinting humanity upon his nature he becomes merely the imprint of his occupation, of his science."[1]

The Adventures of the Spirit

Of all the German idealists, Hegel offers the most thorough treatment of the problem of alienation, especially in that lengthy odyssey of consciousness in search of itself that is *The Phenomenology of Mind*. He believed that alienation was fundamental in life because it is implied in every unfolding of the spirit; it is present whenever man makes an attempt to relate to the objective world. Unlike the world of nature which is fixed, man must strive for unity and harmony through a long labyrinth of negations. The tensions between what we are and what we should ideally be is the basis of Hegel's theory that alienation is the motor force of the dialectical struggle for wholeness. He saw the history of philosophy as a history of "basic contradictions," and the task of philosophy in this present period of disintegration was to "demonstrate the principle that will restore the missing unity and totality."[2]

Lewis Feuer has suggested that Hegel first imbibed the notion of alienation from pessimistic Protestant theology.[3] This is where he initially got a vision of a broken world, of reality split up into hostile opposites. Feuer's opinion is controverted but nonetheless plausible. In 1788 Hegel entered the seminary at Tübingen, and his first writings were on theological themes. They reveal a temperament that is passionate, mystical and speculative. The young Hegel expressed admiration for Greek folk religion, Kant's ethics and the moral beauty of the Gospel. On the other hand, he deplored institutional religion because it threatened the unity of the human personality. Hegel's sensitivity to the "rent harmony" of things was offset by a profound faith in an underlying unity. Specifically, the Christian idea of love seemed to him at this time the answer to alienation. This is what overcomes the "cleavage" between man and the world. Richard Kroner refers to Hegel's "pantheism of love" in this context and goes on to remark that it "had all of the characteristics of his future metaphysic. It aims at a reconciliation of opposites, tries to overcome one-sided rationalism, one-sided emotionalism or one-sided empiricism. It is dialectical in its structure, although its method is not yet dialectical in the strict sense of the word. Hegel still feels that there is no possible logical path to ultimate truth, that a living unity of spiritual experience must take the place of a constructed unity of concepts."[4]

Gradually, however, Hegel came to see the inadequacy of an appeal to religious supports. Reason itself, he became convinced, must fashion a logic that could successfully cope with the antinomies of experience. What Hegel now wanted was a "living logic." Perhaps it would not be too inaccurate to refer to it as a "logic of love" since it would perform the healing, harmony-creating powers that had previously been ascribed to religion. The first statement of this logic appeared in a short work Hegel published in 1801 entitled *The Difference Between the Systems of Fichte and Schelling.* Here he speaks of the "bifurcation" that has come to constitute the essence of man and applies the term to the opposition that characterizes such concepts as spirit and matter, freedom and necessity, reason and sensibility, intelligence and nature, totality and limitation. The basic reason for this state of bifurcation is the externalization of spirit in its cultural expressions, including its "flight to the Deity." Already the dual character of the mind (which is at the basis of Hegel's concept of alienation) is emphasized. In one movement the mind objectifies, divides and separates; concepts are posited as objects set over against it. But at another level, the objects of thought are seen as constitutive of thinking itself, and what was posited as alien is now reunited in a second movement, as the categories of the mind become the categories of being—coextensive with existence itself. What is peculiar about this view is that in positing itself the mind must "lose" itself. This constitutes the dialectic of negation and recovery that is so characteristic of Hegel's thinking. Thus necessary bifurcation and eventual unification is the paradox that philosophy presupposes. The latter's task is completed when the paradox has been dissolved.

The "highway of despair" Hegel speaks of in the *Phenomenology* is a metaphor for the series of negations mind must traverse in pursuit of its own unity. "The existence of this world, as also the actuality of self-consciousness, depends on the process that self-consciousness divests itself of its personality, by so doing creates its world and treats it as something alien and external, of which it must now take possession. . . . To put the matter otherwise, self-consciousness is only something definite, it only has real existence, so far as it alienates itself from itself."[5] Thus consciousness is an Unhappy Consciousness, "the alienated Soul which is the consciousness of self as a divided nature, a doubled and merely contradictory being" (p. 251). Or, again: "Consciousness of life, of its existence and action, is merely pain and sorrow over this existence and action; for therein consciousness finds only consciousness of its opposite as its essence—and of its own nothingness" (p. 252). Mind is intrinsically tragic because it is by nature opposed to itself; two selves are at war with one another. One part of consciousness aspires after its other half in a long, frustrating adventure toward unity. Thus there is a perpetual state of hostility between mind and what is outside of mind. Military language is suitable to describe this predicament. Thus the Unhappy Consciousness is "the unwon unity of two selves . . . to win, then, in this strife against the adversary, is rather to be vanquished. To attain one's goal is rather to lose it in its opposite." Consider the following passage:

> This unhappy consciousness, divided and at variance with itself, must, because this contradiction of its essential nature is felt to be a single consciousness, always have in the one consciousness the other also; and thus must be straightway driven out of each in turn, when it thinks that it has therein attained to the victory and rest of unity. Its true return into itself, or reconciliation with itself, will, however, display the notion of mind endowed with a life and existence of its own, because it implicitly involves the fact that, while being an undivided consciousness, it is a double consciousness. It is itself the gazing of one self-

consciousness into another, and itself is both, and the unity of both is also its own essence; but objectively and consciously it is not yet this essence itself—is not yet the unity of both [p. 251].

Difficult as this language is, it is clear that Hegel conceives of human nature as dual. On the one hand, the self exists in a state of painful contradiction; on the other, the solution is implicit in this very duality. It already belongs to the Unhappy Consciousness "to be one undivided soul in the midst of its doubleness." Hegel conceives human nature to be essentially spirit (*Geist*) and therefore universal rather than particular. We can actualize our essential nature only in unity with the social substance—culture, law, social and political structures, etc. Man's cultural creations are objectified, external versions of his own self and as such so many ways in which he loses his identity and becomes entrapped and fragmented. But because they are alien extensions of the self, they are forms of the spirit seeking its own identity. They are markers along the spirit's path from alienation to dealienation, from particularity to universality. Thus, in losing itself, spirit paradoxically is set on the path of self-discovery.

The disparity between man's essential (i.e. universal) nature and his existential (i.e. particular) condition is overcome, as indeed are all dualities, by the passage of *Geist* through its negative moments, seeking itself in its opposites and eventually returning to itself, thus constituting mind in its concrete historical reality. Mind's reconstruction of the existing order and return to itself through the pursuit of philosophy is tantamount to bringing the dominion of alienation to an end. All forms of being are permeated by an essential negativity and this most basic of all facts determines their content and movement. Existence, as we have indicated, is both alienation and the process by which the subject comes to itself in mastering and comprehending alienation.[6]

The Prodigal Theme

Hegel's idealism may be viewed as an extension of the Renaissance aspiration for divine status. Like Vico, he saw man as a finite principle tending toward the infinite. More broadly, it may be said that a much longer tradition culminates in Hegel's philosophy dating from at least the time of Augustine. His objective idealism found its counterpart in medieval supernaturalism; the idea of self's loss and subsequent recovery is biblical in origin; and by summarizing all the antinomies of human existence under the general rubric of the conflict between subject and object, Hegel connected the nineteenth-century problem with the philosophical one that had dominated European thought since Descartes. Even Hegel's boldest maneuver—the infinitization of reality—was not original. It has precedents in such thinkers as John Scotus Erigena, Bruno and others of pantheistic inclination, although it is true that Hegel's Romanticism gives his thought a special intensity. He set in sharp relief the philosophical character of Romantic idealism by casting the problem of alienation into a dialectic of absence and presence. All moments of alienation (i.e. absence) must be transmuted into a mode of presence; all opposites, distinctions and dualisms must be absorbed into a final unity. The dialectic of absence-presence necessitates the passage of the subject through all the forms of alienation latent between its ground and its world. Consequently, the bent of Hegel's thinking tended to abolish the distinction between the internal and external to emphasize instead the inner unity and dialectical identity between spirit and its existential moments. Too, the traditional distinction between essence and existence is dissolved. Essence together with its externalized forms becomes the subject itself. Thus the intent of the *Phenomenology* is an effort to recover subject to its essence—in the pure formality of its character as self-consciousness, as presence to itself—by way of its existential moments in the life and history of man. The Romantic emphasis here is twofold: the goal of total freedom, a state in which man would be self-willed and in total mastery of himself and, secondly, the glorification of the mind's creative ability. The Romantics made consciousness absolute by assigning it the power to think the world into existence. Thus, for Schopenhauer the world was his "representation of the world." Similarly for Hegel, who, in Sypher's words, "made a conquest of reality by the very act of cognition, which is also an act of appropriation. He gives final sanction to the Cartesian thesis that only what can be thought exists."[7]

Hegel constructed a powerful theoretical framework for the task he set himself. His analysis of the problem of alienation is impressively keen and thorough. But the conditions he set for its solution, the heavy burden he places upon his dialectical machinery, remain puzzling. In the concluding pages of the *Phenomenology* he describes the beautiful soul as "its own knowledge of itself in its pure transparent unity—self-consciousness, which knows this pure knowledge of pure inwardness to be spirit, [it] is not merely intuition of the divine, but the self-intuition of God Himself . . . With absolute knowledge, Spirit has wound up the process of its embodiment." What could this "transparent unity" be? How could man ever hope to attain the self-intuition of God? What is this "purity" Hegel strives for? One wonders why Hegel opted as he did. Why did he make such a bold claim for human potential? Why such an impossibly high price for dealienation? Why did freedom have to be *absolute* freedom and mind *absolute* mind? Part of the answer, it seems to me, is quite obviously his special version of Romantic idealism which infects his whole treatment of alienation at its source. Sartre once wrote in criticism of idealism: "The spider draws things into its web, coats them with its own drivel, and slowly swallows, reducing them to its own nature." The integrity of "things" simply cannot be respected by this kind of idealism. As has been well said, it is essentially impossible to derive the realm of real existence from the reduced realm of consciousness.

But we may inquire further into the sources of Hegel's idealism. I would argue that it derives its absolutistic character from the traditional Judaeo-Christian ethos. I have already indicated how his vision of a broken world and the harmony of love grew out of his early theological concerns. His fondness for triadic distinctions is a carry-over from trinitarian modes of thought; his early religious convictions that God is knowable and that the Spirit leads to truth translated into the omniscience of reason. It is as though he attempted to combine a theistic model with a humanistic faith and then impose the former upon the latter. His mind was Greek, as it were, but his heart was Christian. His theory of alienation is in many ways a secularized version of the doctrine of the Fall and, perhaps more important, he seems to have derived his concept of the eschatological design of world history from the doctrine of the Second Coming. Just as the world lives in sin until the return of Christ, so too do we live in alienation and division until *Geist* passes through and subsumes all in unity.

> The "Kingdom of God" of the philosophy of religion is identical with the "intellectual kingdom" of the history of philosophy, and with the "kingdom of spirit" of phenomenology. Thus philosophy as a whole represents the same reconciliation with reality as does Christianity through the incarnation of God; as the finally comprehended reconciliation, it is philosophical theology. It seemed to Hegel that the "peace of God" was brought about in a rational way through this reconciliation of philosophy with religion.[8]

The whole world vision of German idealism is in many ways reminiscent of the parable of the Prodigal Son.* The father begets a son from whom he will be necessarily separated. If in the classical tradition our first intuition is of being, the Romantic idealists (and it would not be true to the facts to limit them only to Germany) postulated a radically broken world that first impresses itself upon our sensibilities. Perhaps this was a ploy to accommodate a major cultural fact of their world; namely, the omnipresence and inevitability of alienation. But it seems much more likely that it was a position necessitated by their inherited Christian outlook. The Christian first sees the world as fallen and only in a second moment as redeemed. That is why the idealist solution to the problem of alienation

---

* I am indebted to Professor John Anton of Emory University for suggesting this parallel.

was more mythical than scientific. The idealists harked back to Plotinus and religious interpretations of him rather than the earlier Greek tradition. It never seemed to occur to them that the world might be all right, that the problem was in their vision. There is a curious lack of a critical attitude toward their basic assumptions. They never seemed to have really looked at the world as it is but only as they thought it must be. By supposition God (the One, Spirit, Will, Idea, Pneuma or whatever) created the world less than what it ought to be, hence alienated from its essence. He presumably had no choice to create otherwise and since he "cares" he must need be a suffering, anguished God. The suffering of God (epitomized in the death of Christ) is actually a projection of man's capacity to experience alienation under appropriate circumstances of cultural and individual frustration. In any case, it seems clear that the world theories of the nineteenth century (and here we must forget neither Nietzche nor Freud nor the many penetrating sociological works of the latter part of that century) were serious reflections of the all-pervasiveness of alienation. The pattern was in all cases the same: man is to his works and cultural outcomes what God is to his creation. There is cosmic alienation and there is self-alienation. In the course of Western thought, it was the awareness of the dislocation of the framework within which the first form of alienation took place that led to the dislocation of the second. If the world is not a right place to begin with, then it is impossible to feel at home in it. Cosmic and social changes, especially after Descartes and Rousseau, were the real material factors that gave rise to the problems to which philosophers responded. But a theological *parti pris* always generated the problem to begin with. Hegel joins hands with Augustine as a foremost expositor of this dilemma.

"Nothing More Beautiful . . ."

Some confirmation of the foregoing can be found in Hegel's theory of art. Throughout his life he cast envious eyes upon the Hellenic achievement. He believed it represented a happy, but short, marriage between Spirit and the stuff of the concrete world. "Nothing more beautiful can be or become!" he often exclaimed. He saw classical art, Heller notes, "as the spirit's sensuous but, alas, mortal body, as the embodied resolution of the grievous dualism of essence and appearance, of meaning and reality, of content and form."[9] This was art under the aspect of its "highest appointment," wherein sensuous expression is adequate to the idea which inspires it and need not point symbolically beyond itself. In such works reason "stands in quiet and blessedness in bodily form." But Hegel's view of *Geist* precluded the rebirth of such art. Classical art was a thing of the past because Spirit, in its dialectical climb toward the Absolute, can no longer tolerate the confines of sensible incarnation. It is succeeded by Romantic art, whose purpose is to dramatize Spirit's progressive alienation from the materials of the concrete world and thus vindicate the essentially ideal content of this art. When self and the inner life are regarded as having infinite value, the forms of art must abandon balance and harmony and express the churning turmoil of subjectivity. This turmoil is taken to be a higher freedom, less constricted by sensuous embodiment. When Spirit has achieved absolute freedom and the unbounded subjectivity of human inwardness, this form of art will also perish. The predicament is an insoluble one: classical art violated the true nature of the Spirit; Romantic art violates the conditions of art. Spirit will never again be at home in the marketplace of concrete reality. It has, once and for all, negated its sensuous media and will no longer have intercourse with the world. Spirit aspires rather "to find its satisfaction solely in its own indwelling as the true abode of truth."[10]

Discussing Hegel's attitude toward Hellas, Karl Löwith makes these interesting comments: "Man must be able to act as native in what is other and strange in order not to be a stranger to himself in the otherness of the world outside. Hegel saw the Greek way of life as the great prototype of such 'existential indigenousness'—even when his bold acknowledgement of 'what is' forbade all yearning for the past. What makes the educated European feel at home among the Greeks is the fact that they made the world their homeland; they did not seek to go 'above and beyond.' They manipulated, transformed and converted the substantial alien beginnings of their religious and social culture to such an extent that it became essentially their own. And this is just what philosophy is: to be at home with oneself that man may be at home with his spirit, be no stranger to himself."[11] A good illustration of Löwith's point here is the image of the argonauts making their way, painfully but purposefully, toward Ithaca. The Greeks supposed that there are signs in the world for our orientation, thus making it something more than a welter of disconnected events. Reflection could discern a pattern to things and provide a moral purpose. Thus, Plato interprets the world under the master sign of the good and makes of harmony an ethical goal. Man forges a place for himself by relating to the various dimensions of reality through rational effort. Life is not a pilgrimage but an adventure, sustained by a vision of the whole, a conviction of meaning, a sense of order.

So, too, Aristotle, in developing his contextual metaphysics, explains life in terms of unbroken continuities. Man is not some useless passion, dangling hopelessly over the edge of the universe; the senses, memory, experience, imagination, reason and desire are not viewed as warring elements but as expressive of a fundamental rational activity. Classical man could not understand our obsession with alienation. It is a climate of thought that would be quite foreign to him, for unity and order were the structural features of his view of experience. In the end Odysseus is united with Penelope. Perhaps what Hegel admired most of all in the Greeks was a paradigm of philosophical method he could not imitate, a method that sought first and foremost to find out what things were in and of themselves. His own dialectic carried him far beyond the starry fringes of the given world where the spirit loses itself in mystic space. In a paper written while he was still a student entitled "On the Religion of the Greeks and Romans" Hegel said: "The wise men of Greece thought that the deity had endowed every man with means and energies sufficient for his happiness and that it had modeled the nature of things in such a way as to make it possible for true happiness to be obtained by wisdom and human goodness." He was deeply attracted by the Greek ideal of man within whom the moral law is alive, who strives for harmony with nature and reason, unfettered by those institutions that have come to clutter the landscape of freedom.

Since Hegel's time, alienation has functioned as a central concept in our intellectual undertakings. Through Kierkegaard it entered the mainstream of existentialist thought. Marx and other left-wing Hegelians gave it primacy in sociology (and to some extent in religion as well). When it infiltrated psychological and literary modes of thought, its universality was secured. Our overriding concern with alienation is for some an indication that our civilization is crumbling. For example, James Feibleman writes: "For a culture in decline, such as that of modern Europe, what could be more appropriate than to elevate to the first position in reality a neurotic preoccupation by the human subject with the self, in which the typical individual is to be found in full retreat . . . to a world of negative subjective feelings."[12] Feibleman cites the "nit-picking phenomenology" of Husserl, the "extreme subjective preoccupation with pathological symptoms" of the existentialists and the "disguised subjectivism" of linguistic analysis as instances of a cultural collapse. These forms of philosophy, he says, are not about the real world at all. Rather they consist in a "set of various suggestions of how men can retreat from it into themselves as a way of taking refuge from forces with which they feel unable to cope." Marx made a somewhat similar judgment when he said that the traditional philosopher himself was an abstract form of alienated man. In fact, Marx reached the conclusion that the whole history of alienation is nothing more than the "history of the production of abstract thought." There is no doubt that abstraction and alienation are closely related; nor is there any doubt that alienation is in many ways symptomatic of a pathological condition. Many, as did Marx himself, have abandoned the term as a critical tool of description and explanation on the grounds that what can be said with it can be said better without it.

This raises the question of what analytical precision a term like alienation has. I do not see how we can profitably dispense with it because it occupies such a central place in our vocabularies. On the other hand, we should not expect too much of it. Alienation and related concepts have limited value as first-level descriptive categories. In other words, they don't point directly to facts or observable events, at least as these are conventionally understood in scientific theory. They do, it seems to me, have great value at the level of general explanation. A term like alienation enables us to get at general features of experience, social tendencies and patterns of thought. At this level, for example, the concept of alienation permits us to analyze the intellectual climate that gave rise to it, as we have partially done in these pages. It would not do, of course, to fall into the genetic fallacy and assume that by describing the origins of a concept we have thereby given a full account of it even though such a description may be very valuable. But by using the concept in this capacity the historian of ideas can discover interesting connections and areas of investigation that may be well worth going into. I am in the final analysis inclined to regard alienation as an important *ethical* concept, alerting us to significant breaches in the fabric of human experience. As such, it may turn out to be a kind of Ariadne's thread, guiding us out of the labyrinth into the light of moral wholeness.

---

1. Friedrich Schiller, *On the Aesthetic Education of Man, in a Series of Letters*, Reginald Snell, tr. (New Haven, Yale University Press, 1954), p. 40.
2. Herbert Marcuse, *Reason and Revolution* (Boston, Beacon Press, 1963), p. 23.
3. Lewis Feuer, "What is Alienation? The Career of a Concept," *Sociology on Trial*, edited by Maurice Stein and A. Vidich (Englewood Cliffs, Prentice-Hall, 1963), p. 128.
4. See his introduction to Friedrich Hegel, *On Christianity: Early Theological Writings*, T. M. Knox, tr. (New York, Harper Torchbooks, 1948), p. 12. Hegel's overarching concern is to establish a true union between individuals and also between

men and the world. He takes as his model the love that obtains between a man and a woman, especially sexual love which issues into new life. Love overcomes alienation by abolishing all opposition and demanding complete surrender. "Love is indignant if part of the individual is severed and held back as a private property" (p. 306).

5. F. Hegel, *The Phenomenology of Mind*, J. B. Baillie, tr. rev. ed. (London, Macmillan, 1931), p. 514. Jean Hyppolite comments as follows: "Human self-consciousness, which is incapable of thinking itself as a separate cogito, does not find itself but in the world that it builds, in other selves whom it recognizes, and where and in whom it often fails to see itself. But this manner of finding oneself in the other, this objectification is always more or less an alienation, *a loss of self while being at the same time a discovery of self*. Thus objectification and alienation are inseparable and their unity cannot be but the expression of a dialectical tension which one perceives in the very movement of history" (my translation). See his *Etudes sur Marx et Hegel* (Paris, Marcel Rivière, 1955), p. 102.

6. With reference to the relationship between the universal and the particular, it should be pointed out that Hegel did not *intend* the universal to be merely abstract. He wanted it to include particularity and subjectivity as the vine includes its branches. He criticized Plato's *Republic* and Aristotle's "forms" precisely because they bore a merely abstract relation to individuals. From this point of view Hegel anticipates the truth of existentialism and liberal democracy and shows keen appreciation for the flavor of experience. However, he only on occasion followed his own good advice, thus furnishing grounds for the charge of idealism. Marx followed Feuerbach in characterizing this idealism as "the apotheosis of abstraction which 'alienates man from himself' because it inverts the real relation of thought to the world. Instead of seeing that the Absolute Idea is itself derived from particular experienced things, Hegel derived particular experienced things from the Absolute Idea. Hence the essence of nature was outside nature, the essence of man outside man, and the essence of thought outside the thinking act." (See Loyd Easton, "Alienation and History in the Early Marx," *Philosophy and Phenomenological Research*, December, 1961, p. 196.) In accepting this criticism one should bear in mind that it does not always apply, particularly to Hegel's political writings.

□ *THE ADVENT OF ALIENATION*

7. Wylie Sypher, *Literature and Technology: The Alien Vision* (New York, Random House, 1968), p. 141.
8. Karl Löwith, *From Hegel to Nietzsche*, David Green, tr. (New York, Doubleday, 1967), pp. 324–25.
9. Erich Heller, *The Artist's Journey into the Interior* (New York, Random House, 1966), p. 114.
10. *Ibid.*, p. 117.
11. Karl Löwith, *op. cit.*, p. 165.
12. James Feibleman, "The History of Philosophy as a Philosophy of History," *The Southern Journal of Philosophy*, Winter 1967, pp. 275 ff.

Part III

THE

END OF

ALIENATION?

The question of how the reign of alienation may be brought to an end is the most urgent question of our time. Many proposals have been put forth and indeed there are bold spirits who have argued that we have already entered the era of dealienation. Marcus Klein, for example, finds that the most serious novelists in America since mid-century have moved beyond the deep sense of malcontentedness reflected in the work of their predecessors.[1] Accommodation rather than alienation, he says, best describes the mood reflected in these novelists; they have shed "the sense of separate and unconciliating identity" in order to move toward "affirmation of ordinary life in the world, to functional activity in the community." The period between the two wars, on the other hand, was a time of dissatisfaction, iconoclasm and rebellion. Society was the enemy. The term "alienation" appropriately describes the spirit which during the twenties and thirties animated the great social and literary assaults on an intolerable status quo. The large achievements of those years mitigated the pain of alienation. After World War II the mood shifts; the sense of loss is no longer adequately descriptive of the writer's predicament, no longer what Klein calls a relevant intellectual position. "The revolution in behalf of an alienated engagement found itself ancient, respectable, and irrelevant to the social reality." The postwar novelists, Mailer most conspicuously, could not successfully maintain a pose of alienation. They smashed away fruitlessly at already fallen idols and confused their private affairs with public issues of great moment.

161

□ THE AGE OF ALIENATION

The new stance of accommodation was born partly of the exhausted vein of deep discontent that had earlier made alienation a persuasive term of social criticism and partly of new social circumstances. It is characterized by a certain confrontation of self and society in which individual freedom finds objective reference in social need. For example, today there is the kind of organized protest against injustices that can provide an outlet for the artist's sense of outrage and at the same time inspire his work with a less alienated, more adapted tone. Accommodation is consequently a more ambiguous term. The distinctions between rebellion and cooperation, engagement and disengagement, self and society are less sharply drawn. The alienated writer spoke out passionately and clearly; good and evil were readily recognizable. His successor is less sure; his adjustment is never more than tentative, his prose is less energetic; the ebb and flow of his convictions make his presence a muted one. There is a cruel irony in this. When our sense of evil has become obscured, the evil itself increases, if for no other reason than that we are less able to combat it. The era of accommodation in this sense is no improvement over the era of alienation. In Klein's words:

> The culture is now without doubt still less habitable for the artist-intellectual, or anyone else, than it was. The boobs are gone, but replaced by the arrogant middlebrows, the *fonctionnaires,* of the Media. Dayton, Tennessee, is replaced by Little Rock and Birmingham. An imposing Puritanism has been sublimed into IBM machinery. A cruel industrialism has been replaced by a rampant scientism. And meanwhile the nation's creative energies are given to sport, the famous race with the Russians . . . [p. 295].

After Alienation was published in 1962. Today we would have to add Vietnam, the space race and ecological imbalance. The evil is greater and our means of combating it proportionately reduced. Thus the irony remains. But accommodation also marks a hope and despite everything asserts the possibility of a viable human community. This, Klein concludes, is the ultimate theme of the literature of accommodation. "It is a literature that exists between the extremes of an easy nihilism and a bland hopefulness . . . because there, between those extremes, is where the humanity that is to be asserted goes on. Accommodation is restoration and love in their ordinary, domestic, painfully contingent instances and it makes up in plain necessity what it lacks in conscience" (p. 296).

Is Klein's distinction between alienation and accommodation merely a verbal one? I think not. It is by no means a vigorous distinction but there is perhaps just enough importance in it to point the problem of alienation toward a more promising resolution. It allows for involvement, the testing of self-powers against the evils to be overcome, in a way the older term did not. For it is a fact that today increasing numbers are demanding a redress of justice, a righting of society's infamy and man's inhumanity to man; they are actively striving for fuller freedom and a more humane existence. This is obviously true of students, Negroes and the poor (primarily in South America); but also joined in the fight are increasing numbers of clergymen, artists and writers, professors, jurists and even businessmen. There is in the making something like a world coalition of consciences against the forces of alienation. Humanity does indeed go on in this struggle; insofar as the ordinary conditions of existence are becoming those outposts of contact between felt human needs and organized steps toward their resolution, accommodation is a helpful rubric under which to view the thrust toward reconstruction and redefinition. But we must at the same time bear in mind that the distinction does little more than refocus the problem; it offers no programmatic content or concrete guidelines. Still, the direction is there, the hope is offered. "The context is history moving toward the light of consciousness." Pound's line, perhaps, encapsulates the spirit of accommodation. Alienation is the generating force of its own dissolution; its solution lies within history. Insofar as Klein's distinction alerts us to this it is a useful one.

A Spirit in Search of a Substance

Let us now consider another way in which the end of alienation has been envisaged. In a stimulating volume entitled *Beyond Alienation* Ernest Becker has advanced the thesis that a philosophy of education based on a theory of alienation would lead to a new moral view of the world and thus end the long history of human estrangement.[2] In other words, to put forth a coherent and compelling theory of human ills is at the same time to state how they shall be overcome. The answer to the question, Why do people act as they do? will be a prescription for the end of alienation. Becker puts it this way:

> Is there any answer to the incredible world-picture of the twentieth century? Is there something that can work against the death grip of both commercial and communist ideology, and mechanistic science and maybe even history itself? One thing perhaps—one thing alone: a theory of alienation, a broad and compelling theory, which showed what man was, what he was striving for,

and what hindered this striving—in himself, in society, in nature. We need a theory of alienation that was composed of the best knowledge in psychology, sociology, ontology, and theology, and this is what the hard-pressed human spirit itself supplied. It was a theory of alienation that was at the same time a thoroughgoing new moral view of the world [p. 227].

Becker believes this breakthrough came in the eighteenth century. In fact he claims that the eighteenth century discovered the problem of alienation and formulated a complete program for overcoming it. Although he claims too much here, his emphasis is a correct one. We have already spoken about how Rousseau and others explored the social dimension of alienation and counteracted the Newtonian world-outlook with something like a "science of man." The concerns of Enlightenment thinkers did very often turn to a consideration of how human energies and freedom might best be realized. Becker therefore has good reason to remind us of what they wrote about "the constraints placed upon man by the state of civilization, the blunting of natural passions and appetites, the frustration of natural desires, the twisting and corrupting of basic needs." Theirs was "a quest for an answer to the problem of how exactly society caused human unhappiness. It was our debate, the one we are still airing and struggling to define" (p. 92).

One reason why it is still very much our debate is that we have not built on the eighteenth-century foundations, we have not, as it were, fleshed out the "ideal concept" of alienation, so that after two centuries it is still "a spirit in search of a substance." What we must now do is convert alienation "into a broad picture of human failure" in order to see how society constricts human energies and begin the task of social reconstruction. This would involve a program of education in which our best empirical data is brought to bear on three levels of understanding: the individual, the socio-historical and the philosophico-theological. At the first level the law of the individual's unfolding would be explained: how alienation arises out of his own development; how we are born into a social milieu and trained in a predetermined mold of values, how the sense of freedom awakens when struck against the anvil of determinism; how self-reliance can overcome self-estrangement; how self-knowledge can come to predominate over the ignorance and psychological disadvantages into which we are born, and so forth. The psychological disciplines provide the essential data at this level of education. Becker's position is that our knowledge of human development must be oriented around the law of the Oedipus complex. In this way we can best show how a child's anxiety over object-loss disposes him to forfeit self-powers and follow the personhood patterns of his parents and environing society. What has to be uncovered if alienation is to be overcome are the inauthentic ways in which we accept uncritically the meanings that govern our lives. Hopefully, a thorough education at this level would expose the evils that are a result of "weakness, of narrow, inflexible, frightened, clumsy, ineffective life styles." These are the evils that cause alienation.

At the socio-historical level the program of education would concentrate on such questions as what societies are, how they come to be historically, how they function, how they change, etc. This is the domain of sociology, anthropology, history, political science, economics and literature. The underlying assumption at this level of the program is that self-knowledge and knowledge of ourselves as performers on the stage of culture are closely related. Of the many important issues that must come under consideration at this juncture, foremost is the question of what is authentic and what is artificial (and destructive of human powers) in society. For example, what does bureaucracy do to man? Weber predicted the day when a mechanical bureaucratic society would become a great iron cage drowning out every sound but that of its own hum. Have we reached that day? Another important question is: How comes it that history has led to such inequality among men? What has gone unexamined here that permits the perpetuation of such a state of affairs? How has the human spirit been trapped by history? What we want to know, in the final analysis, is how society generates and imposes values, and what norms of judgment would enable man to discriminate among these values. How can man be critical in an uncritical society?

Such questions lead to the final dimension of the "alienation curriculum." We must in the end form some philosophical estimate of what man ideally can be. Various other disciplines can tell us what he *is* but this knowledge is of no avail unless we know what to do with it. To provide this criterion Becker elaborates what he calls a naturalistic ontology. How does man's life achieve maximum meaning and conviction? We know at this point that uncritical acceptance is what forces our life energies into shallow channels, what Becker calls "narrow types of aesthetic mergers." We know that the problem is rooted in man's fear of establishing autonomous meanings, that this is the weakness society grows around. But what is the answer? Becker's ontology leads him to conclude that man is a meaning creating animal. He views him as an energetic organism and defines meaning as "the relationships between things controlled and understood by the experiencing organism." And he goes on to say that "when experience is integrated the life force attains its highest intensity and when this intensity is fused completely with nature, via the aesthetic object, life attains its highest truth and reality . . . Human life is a groping for an aesthetics of total satisfaction." Imagination is the key faculty here. It is the power which draws upon energies within us, frees us from the mold of habit and convention and enables us to create a scheme of adequate meanings. The paradox of human development, as Becker sees it, is this: creative meanings can only come from individuals but individuals don't want to step out from the herd. Consequently "the one animal in nature who is a potentially open vehicle for the life force actually closes up that vehicle by his fear of standing on his own original meanings." The transference from an uncritical stance to one of seeing the world in light of appropriated meanings calls for radical reconstruction—a thorough knowledge of what causes our ills on the one hand and a suitable ideal of freedom on the other. Ultimately, human freedom becomes a theological question, for theology is the discipline that tells us what freedom is for.*

Becker's program has much to recommend it. What I find particularly attractive is his central thesis that knowledge will make us whole. This updated version of the Socratic teaching that virtue is knowledge gives us an important weapon in our struggle against those evils that are man-made and man-curable. Furthermore, it shifts the emphasis away

* Becker is perhaps too enthusiastic about the role of theology. A statement like "God alone can make sense of a free horizon of meaning" itself raises serious problems of meaning. There is some rhetorical appeal in charging that modern man whines under the burden of life because "he has nothing ultimate to dedicate it to; nothing infinite to assume responsibility for; nothing self-transcending to be truly courageous about. He has only himself, his dazzling and diverting little consumer objects; his few closely huddled loved ones; his life-span; his life-insurance; his place in a merely biological and financial chain of things." But if anything is clear to me from reading the history of ideas it is that dedication to ultimate and infinite principles of self-transcendence has been a primary cause of alienation rather than a cure for it.

from the raw voluntarisms that infect our educational psychology. Little of what Becker proposes is going on in present educational programs. The model he sketches could be profitably initiated. At this point, however, I want to give the discussion a critical turn. First of all, I am not altogether happy with the logic of the belief that because we know what causes our troubles we will be able to come up with a cure. Knowing, for example, that our herd instinct is rooted in anxiety isn't of itself going to dispel the anxiety or make us more devoted to autonomous meanings. Instead of arguing, as Becker does, that a comprehensive theory of alienation carries its own solution, I would say that this constitutes the first important step toward a solution.

Secondly, and more importantly, there is an aspect of the eighteenth-century "discovery" of alienation Becker does not deal with. I refer to the myth of progress we have inherited from that era which, on my view, must be recognized as an important part of the problem of alienation. As has been humorously said, progress is what people who are planning to do something terrible almost always justify themselves on the grounds of.[3] Man's value perspective was substantially altered by the prestige this myth attained in the eighteenth and nineteenth centuries and, as I shall presently be concerned to point out, not for the best. The way the concept of progress has affected our sense of time is one way it has intensified our awareness of alienation. By stressing the dynamic and vital, the yet to be, we have come to value future possibilities over present needs. The focus of our energies under a theory of progress is not present enjoyments but eventual fulfillment. Northrop Frye has well pointed out that the sacrifice of the present to the future is a modern version of Moloch-worship, a mere Juggernaut. He further notes that as a result of this dislocation of time "our emotional relation to the future becomes one of dread and uncertainty. The future is the point at which 'it is later than you think' becomes 'too late.' Modern fiction has constantly dealt, during the last century, with characters struggling toward some act of consciousness or self-awareness that would be a gateway to real life."[4] This goal, we might add, is almost never reached.

The myth of progress has also contributed to our awareness of alienation by virtue of the autonomy it assumes and the consequent loss of human control. Social progress in democratic countries has been one example of this; or the autonomous character of historical development in Marxist ideology. Systems become self-perpetuating and impervious to constructive criticism or human needs. Let me illustrate this by the following example. There is in Africa a species of caterpillar that instinctively follows nose-to-tail any other member of its kind it happens to encounter. Frequently long parades of them are found moving slowly across roads or village paths. Upon occasion the leader will come upon the last in a line. When this happens the first one tails in behind the last, and the whole line goes round in a circle until the food supply on its track is exhausted. Then they all die. One might ask if we are not creeping nose-to-tail in a social system of such vast complexity that we cannot see that it is going nowhere, in which every element in the system is balanced off by other elements in such a way that the system itself has an unshakable stability, a resistance to change and criticism so great that when it dies it will have to be buried whole. Our social structures dangerously resemble such a circle of caterpillars. It often seems that there are no people in them, no villains or heroes, only abstract faces assimilated by the system, playing out the undrama in a pointless way. Each of us can think of countless examples from the current scene of events. What the system requires is not criticism or appropriated meanings but continuity and uniformity as the deadening pilgrimage wends toward some hope lost in the dim recesses of the future*

The Eclipse of Ethics

I come now to my third point of criticism. The myth of progress has been most conspicuously linked to science and technology. Becker says that the eighteenth century gave us a new moral view of the world. He also admits that this view is still a spirit in search of a substance and that the time has come to enter the land promised by the new moral view. But there is a serious ambiguity here. The reason why this view did not prevail in the eighteenth century is the same reason why it is not likely to prevail in the twentieth century; namely, because morality was subsumed by the scientific outlook, so much so that ever since that time we have looked to science for our moral direction. We still do. After the success of Apollo 11, to take a recent instance, there was much talk about the event as a moral achievement —triumph of middle-class morality, etc. This tendency to extrapolate lessons of moral import from technological achievements (and the accomplishment of Apollo 11, wondrous indeed, was at bottom different only in degree from the invention of the wheel) ignores the defining characteristic of our culture: the astonishing gap between the success of scientific method and our ethical disorientation, our inability to meet the most elementary moral demands. As W. H. Auden put it, ourselves still don't fit us exactly. This is the myth of progress in scientific guise—the assumption

---

*I am indebted to my colleague Dr. Daniel Anderson for the "caterpillar theory."

that we are moving inevitably from slavery to freedom, from the dark of superstition into the light of a new dawn.

No one is likely to deny that science and technology can improve the moral condition of man. There is always some ethical spin-off from science. But just as often the reverse is the case. And in any event, the point to be stressed is that science is ethically neutral. A while back, Emmanuel Mesthene wrote that "our technical prowess literally bursts with the promise of a new freedom, enhanced human dignity and unfettered aspiration." He could as convincingly have written that our technical prowess leads to slavery and literally bursts with the threat of destruction. Technology of itself does not bring an increase in human freedom nor does science undirected automatically point toward paradise. The modern positivist's faith is as deep and touching as that of any medieval mystic. But it cannot go unexamined. The point I want to make is that our characteristic uses of intelligence today are not directed toward ethical ends. Quite the contrary. Scientific method is committed to a cerebral mode of thought, biased in favor of the quantifiable and measurable. As Whitehead said, it seeks a universality that is a disconnection from immediate surroundings. In order to get what he is seeking, the scientist must abstract from and to that extent distort the experienced world. Yet this world does not immediately present itself in the form of the abstract or quantifiable. The chemical formula of water, for example, tells us nothing about the experience of slaking one's thirst. No one would want to argue that water is merely H_2O or that this formula is the whole or even the most important truth about water. Scientific truth is a de-limited, fragmentary truth. A certain portion of reality is isolated and inspected from a specialized viewpoint.

Thus it follows that scientific truth can only be scientifically meaningful. What is directly felt and immediately valued by men—i.e. the qualitative dimension of experience—is relegated to a position of inferior status if not in fact condemned to unreality, thus bearing out the positivist dogma that that which cannot be the object of exact observation, of scientific analysis, of measurement and experimental verification is unknowable. It is an article of faith that we can speak intelligently about what is empirically verifiable but not about what is good or valuable. To summarize the ideology of scientific method as briefly as possible, we may say that science in and of itself has no moral dimension whatsoever; it discerns no values in the world it investigates. The latter—whether religious, aesthetic or ethical—are shunted onto the non-cognitive sidings of the intellectual enterprise. Thus, no rational discussion about values is possible; these belong to the realm of the unverifiable and serve no other purpose than to indicate our emotional states. As Stanley Rosen has said, scientific reason has become detached from its traditional affiliation with the conception of the good. "Reason modelled on mathematics alienates, reifies, objectifies; it debases and destroys the genuinely human. It obscures the significance of human existence by superimposing the rigid, inhuman and, in the last analysis, man-made categories of mathematized ontology . . . Man has become alienated from his own authentic and creative existence by the erroneous projection of an arithmological domain of beings (and so of an autonomous technology) which is the contemporary historical manifestation of rationalism."[5] In a word, the self has been so severely abstracted from the full range of human experience that authenticity has become virtually impossible. Science enables us to do a great many things. But it cannot tell us what is worth doing. It is incapable of dealing with the meaning problems of life or bringing us face to face with ourselves in any mode of self-knowledge.

This is a familiar enough charge. What we perhaps advert to less frequently is that the consequence has been an almost total eclipse of ethics. It has become either impossible, irrelevant or simply uninteresting to raise the prime moral questions because there is no viable context within which we might answer them. What is the good life? What are the desirable possibilities of human activity? How can we realize them? What concept of human excellence might adequately draw out the highest potential of contemporary man? How ought one to act in order to give life the meaning it fundamentally ought to have? Who is the good man in contemporary society and how would we recognize him if we met him? We simply don't know. We clutch at any hope from whatever quarter. When it gets right down to it, we have no reliable criteria for identifying what is authentically worth pursuing, no way of settling ethical priorities. Few of us have tested convictions concerning the good, the just, the beautiful; no vital sense of the distinction between what is desired and what is desirable, between the authentic and the meritricious. Thus, it is all very well to say that we *could* clean up the cities if we redirected the flow of monies from, say, the Vietnam war or the space program. Of course we could. But what power, what standard, shall determine this priority? In the end the goals of human activity are set by a destructive amalgam of convention, dire emergency, economic gain and the dictates of a value-free scientism.* Man is the loser. Archibald MacLeish recently spoke of "the diminished man"

---

* Lest these remarks be interpreted as anti-science, let me hasten to point out that I am talking about the *abuse* of a method. I agree with Bernard Boelen when he writes that 'no scientific method can be absolutized without distorting the fundamental structure of human existence, no scientific method can be ignored without atrophying truly human possibilities . . . Not science is to be blamed for the impoverishment of human ex-sistence which has caused the crisis of our present age, but *scientism* or the absolutism of the exact methods of thinking." It is not science as such which leads to human impoverishment but "the monistic acceptance of one method to the exclusion of every other method." (See his *Existen-*

in this context. Our inability to direct human resources into morally enriching channels, he reasoned, has resulted in that "anesthesia of the soul" that permeates all our cultural structures. The eclipse of ethics and the diminishment of man go hand in hand.

When we probe deeper into this moral vacuum we discover that what has been basically eclipsed in any sense of the centered self that our traditional humanisms have always assumed to be the source and guarantor of values. Such a self construes its identity by organizing experience as a coherent and integral structure. When man's activity is directed toward rationally secured ideals, he performs most adequately as a moral agent and comes upon an affirmative answer to the meaning of life. In the final analysis the traditional humanisms held the good life to consist in man's ability to shape the materials of his experience in light of credible principles of self-realization. Plato was the first to work out this principle. The role of reason is to unify the self in a condition of harmony such that each faculty performs its proper function in unison with the personality as a whole. Justice is the over-arching virtue which guarantees this harmony of functions. In the *Republic* Plato writes: "Righteousness pertains to the inner action not the outer, to oneself and to the elements of the self, restricting the specific elements in one's self to their respective roles, forbidding the types in the psyche to get mixed up in one

---

tial Thinking, Pittsburgh, Duquesne University Press, 1968, p. 97.) I protest those aspects of our technological order which serve violence and waste and dull the moral sense. Our most urgent problems today are ethical rather than scientific in nature. I plead for a recognition of this fact and urge the restoration of an ethical court of appeal beyond science. Until this has taken place there is no answer to questions like: How can we control technology? Or render it more humanitarian, a less autocratic and totalitarian endeavor? The point is that a large body of our scientific knowledge is premature; it outstrips our ability to synthesize and assign it its proper place in the spectrum of human wisdom.

another's business; requiring a man to make a proper disposition of his several properties and to assume command of himself and to organize himself and become a friend of himself . . . becoming in all respects a single person instead of many." This is the original, deep sense of "doing one's thing."

Socrates stands as a classic embodiment of this ideal, an incomparable example of man living excellently. Often in the dialogues Plato has Socrates withdraw from the argument to confer with his *daimon*. The modern reader often misses the significance of this ploy, regarding it as a mythic carry-over or a merely literary device. But when Socrates turned to his *daimon* he was in fact testing the many opinions disclosed in dialogue against what he profoundly felt. It was a technique by means of which he authenticated truth on the smithy of an integrated self. Thus, when he took a stand, as he did most eminently against his accusers, it was one that was secured not only by the soundest of arguments but was also consonant with his undivided personality. It was not only truth but his truth. Hegel called Socrates one of those great plastic figures, all of a piece, who "form themselves completely into what they are." The final test of their excellence is neither argument, nor the will of the state nor the voice of the oracles. It is the centered self. This is what must essentially underlie social systems and ideologies and serve as the ultimate point of moral reference. Socrates knew that it, rather than expediency, was the only defense against the alienating influences that populate the world. Thus was he able to draw together the multiple aspects of his experience for action and well-being. He welded knowledge and conviction into a clear discernment of what was best for man in society. This is the meaning of the Socratic formula that virtue is knowledge. To know truly who one is and the reasons why one acts is the good life.

□ THE END OF ALIENATION?

No such virtue unifies modern man's activity. As Nietzsche (and Rousseau before him) saw, the determining quality of modern life is the strange contrast between an inner life to which nothing outward corresponds and an outward existence unrelated to what is within. Today, the self, insofar as we can speak of such an entity at all, is represented as an absence, a locus of insurmountable contradictions, a shifting universe of conflicting interests. Sartre and a great chorus of contemporary thinkers chime in unison that the nature of man is to have no nature! "Each turbid turn of the world has such disinherited children." Rilke's line aptly suggests the splintered outcomes of disconnected pursuits. The fragmented self, quite obviously, cannot be centered—morally or any other way. This, I take it, is the basis of our contemporary mythologies of wastelands and one-dimensionality. It is at the very core of our current preoccupation with the alienation of man. Our most prevalent self-images grow out of the soil of shattered cogitos. The modern self is a plural entity that can be identified chiefly by the roles it plays, often enough with little regard for their contradictory character; it ventures forth on many roads of promised fulfillments, and like a camp-follower, pledges fidelity to many suitors. Conduct is segmentalized; our vocabularies divide and sub-divide like amoebas. No consistent self-image emerges from our lavish output of energy. This ability to play multiple roles attests to modern man's flexibility, a quality that enables him to accommodate the demands made upon him by a technological society. But at the same time it denies consistency and wholeness as the basis of ethical conduct. It precludes determinate character as a mark of moral excellence. No *daimon* presides over modern man's multi-faceted existence.

Two objections might be lodged against my position at this point. The first would be to argue that science and technology are not at all inimical to ethical excellence. One form of this argument is advanced by those naturalistic humanists (including utilitarians and pragmatists) who hold that values can be empirically warranted, that cultural relativism is consistent with a healthy objectivity, that scientific knowledge alone can solve the problems of men, including their moral problems. They hold, in other words, that ethical judgments are objective and empirically testable. The scientific humanist, as we may call him, rejects the necessity of trans-empirical justification for morality. He claims that ethical norms or ideals are rooted in observable human needs and behavior, and that there are scientifically evident features of the development of the human race and of individuals that bear directly on moral theory. Proponents of this school reason that the challenge before us is to apply to moral matters the kind of method that accounts for the stunning successes of science, and many of them reason very persuasively for this viewpoint. This is especially so when the argument is supplemented with insights from the psychological disciplines. Rollo May, for example, has long called for a "science of man" based on what he takes to be man's distinguishing characteristics: e.g. man the symbol maker, the reasoner, the historical mammal who can participate in his community and who possesses the potentiality for freedom and ethical action. The pursuit of such a science, May notes, will place the scientific enterprise in a broader context, and he expresses the hope that it will become possible, when our current conceptions of "objective truth" have been exploded, to study man scientifically and still see him whole. That day may come. But for the moment the positivist denial of any "scientific" status for ethics has carried the day.

A stronger form of the same objection contends that

science and technology will bring about a radical transformation in man such that all ethical matters will of necessity become a matter of technological control. Victor Ferkiss, for example, summarizes this position in his recent book *Technological Man.* We stand, he pointed out, on the threshold of self-transfiguration, a new species of man; we have, or shortly will have, the power to alter radically the meaning and character of human existence. Ferkiss sees the electronic transformation of our environment and the impact of the life sciences as most indicative of the possibility of a new species. At the deepest level of human existence, he writes, man as we have known him is on the verge of becoming something else. A new concept of the structured self, now no longer dependent on decision and freedom, will emerge. In truth, this possibility contains no logical contradiction. If it comes to pass, discussions such as this one will be altogether beside the point. Then ethics will have suffered a different and definitive kind of eclipse, even though such a prospect does nothing to remedy our present situation. Nor does it cast any light on the deeper problem of what criteria shall be used to program the new man. Even though we should attain the power of determining our natures, how shall we determine what we want to be?

The second objection is essentially iconoclastic in nature and views any approach to ethical vitality that is based on the concept of a structured self as hopelessly anachronistic, far from the thrust of modern man's creativity. The iconoclastic mentality cares nothing for the past, the achieved, the remembered. It has no belief in the nature of things. Agitated by constant change, by what Benjamin DeMott has called the prodding demons of possibility, it bends every effort to smash ancient stabilities, including the notion of an ethical center. Iconoclasm is perhaps most obviously manifested in the ideology of revolution. But, more deeply, it is woven into the very fabric of the contemporary mind-set. In poetry, painting, drama—indeed in all our cultural expressions—the traditional sense of structure has given way to the emergence of more fluid, open-ended forms. "I am my freedom," says Orestes in Sartre's *The Flies*. "I am doomed to have no other law but mine. There is no one to give me orders." Such a hero has no ties with nature, with society, with others. Life for him is always a clean slate, a series of virgin beginnings. "All here is new, all must begin anew . . ." Earl Rovit calls this phenomenon an expression of the contemporary apocalyptic imagination. The proven centers of the past, he states, cannot contain the energies our age has released. The imagination must relocate the basis of moral action by redefining or, better, eliminating the self. The new images of meaning and identity are explosive, ephemeral and disconnected, as in a Fellini movie. As Rovit puts it: "The apocalyptic ethic utters a challenging command: 'Distrust thyself!' it says. 'Trust rather to thy congeries of selves. Look to the peripheries of thy being for that is where life exists, not in some hollow center.' "[6] Thus does contemporary iconoclasm celebrate the liberation of the self from all fixed boundaries.

This mentality, however, is by no means as contemporary as it is thought to be. It is in fact only a slightly modified version of the Renaissance ethic of infinite fulfillment we discussed earlier. The Renaissance gave decisive impetus to that peculiarly modern bias of favoring the possible over the actual, the future over the past, processes over products, the fluid over the fixed. This is basically a Faustian attitude: infinite striving, the inability to rest at any point of completion, is taken to be a mark of what is divine in man. Whence the many attempts in our day to create a "new reality."

I want to make it clear that I have no quarrel with the emphasis on process as such. As I shall indicate shortly, it provides an important clue to the nature of experience. What I want to stress is the time-conditioned limitations of our faculties. Total openness to the future, to all possibilities is humanly impossible. We can only indulge in this kind of indeterminacy at the price of never becoming anything at all. To be all things potentially often means no more than being nothing. Adventuring randomly among alternative life styles is in the final analysis adolescent and counterproductive—the way of the anti-hero, a Prufrock idly postponing decision until another time. The contemporary celebration of peripheral being ends in enslavement to pointless change and the immediately given. It dooms us to perpetual reconstructions. When one happening has ended, there is nothing to do but begin another. When a new line of consumer goods is announced, the nation convulses toward immediate possession. Experience thus arranged *seriatim* falsely assumes that ethical authenticity obtains when life is impregnated with challenges and changes, when human resources are animated by a perpetual crisis of transition. Without a sustaining vision of the good life, a stable point of reference, we lack that fulcrum of self-affirmation that is the necessary basis of any morality.

Toward the Unity of Experience

What alienation comes to, after all, is the fragmentation of experience. From this point of view it may be considered primarily the moral question of how to unify experience. This supposes, of course, that we have some theory of what experience is. Unfortunately (and this is no small part of the problem of alienation), the West has only fitfully been concerned with the nature of experience. The Greeks made a good beginning—from the naturalism of the early Ionians through the almost sexual rhythm of Socrates' dialectic and Plato's aesthetic conception of experience to Aristotle's rich biologism. It was, as a matter of fact, a very good beginning. But the Greek achievement was largely dissolved in the mystic view of experience that dominated the Middle Ages and still lingers on effectively in modern idealism—whether rationalist, Romantic or existentialist. Common to all mystic interpretations of experience is the assumption that its real core is in some superior region beyond ordinary existence— in God, empyrean Reason, innate ideas, a priori concepts, or wherever. In all these cases ordinary experience is considered intrinsically defective, something to be transcended and completed in some realm beyond itself. Idealisms always end by reducing experience to a mode of supra-sensible knowing. The empirical concept of experience that we associate with the tradition of Bacon, Locke and Hume launched a sustained criticism against this tradition with its reliance on abstraction and tendency to mysticism and made a not wholly unsuccessful attempt to repatriate our ideas in the sensed world. The main shortcoming of the empiricists was their view that sense experience is composed of atomistic elements that are passively received by the mind; that it was no more than the finished fact presented in isolated fashion to intelligence. Because of its emphasis on the singular and discrete, empiricism could discern no *connection* among the parts of experience and as a result was in the end even less successful than idealism in its attempt to unify experience.* Paradoxical as it may seem, the best philosophies of experience have been articulated by American thinkers.

*Cf. supra, p. 65.

182

□ THE END OF ALIENATION?

Already in Peirce and George Herbert Mead the "subjectivism" of traditional concepts of experience was strenuously opposed. In Peirce's theory of cosmic evolution, for example, we have a sketch of a theory of experience that is impressively more comprehensive and able to account for the generic traits of existence. Mead's emphasis falls upon social experience. He worked out a theory of interaction between living organisms and the whole environment. He saw alienation as a form of disorganization that resulted from man's isolation from meaning in his work, his institutions and his community—disruptions that in turn resulted from the social and technological innovations of modern times. Mead's fundamental insight is sometimes characterized as a "bio-social behaviorism," according to which minds and selves emerge dynamically from a social matrix.

In such thinkers as James, Dewey and Whitehead we have much more fully articulated theories of experience. Their main interest was to work out a coherent, inter-related account of all elements of our experience. Thus Whitehead's "philosophy of organism," his emphasis on the categories of "connectedness" and "creativity" were attempts to restore life and value to a privileged place among our concerns, an emphasis that was conspicuously lacking from the cosmological scheme of the Newtonian tradition. He defined his philosophy as an endeavor "to frame a coherent, logical, necessary system of general ideas in terms of which every element of our experience can be interpreted."[7] James was also getting at an organic philosophy, largely through psychological channels. The parts of experience, he held, "hold together from next to next by relations that are themselves parts of experience. The directly apprehended universe needs, in short, no extraneous trans-empirical connective support, but possesses in its own right a concatenated or continuous structure."[8] James's model for his concept of experience was the processes of consciousness. Consciousness has its own inner logic and powers of structuring and connecting, its own mode of interaction. By examining consciousness pragmatically, James was led to an important conclusion about the nature of truth, namely, that it is what unifies experience, getting one part into satisfactory relationships with all other parts. He further concluded that the experience of self-identity as well as the meaning of the world are to be found in the relational interaction between self and environment.

Dewey built on this insight and, I believe, offers the best theory of experience yet elaborated. All his life he fought narrow disruptive dualisms wherever he found them (and, needless to say, he found a good many of them in traditional philosophical systems). It may fairly be said that the dominant theme of Dewey's writings was the continuous and interdependent quality of life in all of its aspects. When he was a young man he was much impressed by the holistic approach he found in the works of Thomas Huxley. He wrote then of his desire for a world and a life that would have the same properties as the human organism did in Huxley's thought. Hegel and Darwin were two other important influences who helped the young Dewey develop his theory of "organic coordination." Hegel's thought, he wrote,

> supplied a demand for unification that was doubtless an intense emotional craving and yet was a hunger that only an intellectualized subject matter could satisfy. It is more than difficult, it is impossible, to recover that early mood. But the sense of divisions and separations that were, I suppose, borne in upon me as a consequence of a heritage of New England culture, divisions by way of isolation of self from the world, of soul

> from body, of nature from God, brought a pain-
> ful oppression—or, rather, they were an inward
> laceration . . . Hegel's synthesis of subject and
> object, matter and spirit, the divine and the
> human . . . operated as an immense release, a
> liberation.[9]

The category that emerged as basic in Dewey's thought, and toward the clarification of which he directed his intellectual energy, was that of experience. The fresh challenge to serious thought in our time, Dewey remained convinced, was to inseminate all modes of experience with intelligent direction. In this way he hoped the grievous alienations that afflict twentieth-century man could be overcome.

One example of this conviction was his unflagging effort to overcome the dichotomy between science and human affairs. As he said in *The Quest for Certainty* and repeated many times over: "The problem of restoring integration and cooperation between man's beliefs about the world in which he lives and his beliefs about the values and purposes that should direct his conduct is the deepest problem in modern life." The prevailing view that the truths of science and the propositions of ethics have no common intellectual ground made no sense to him. He countered by situating all forms of experience—feeling, desiring and willing, as well as thinking—within nature. Thus our needs and desires are as indicative of what is "natural" as are the discoveries of science; they are not alien to the existential world. This principle of Dewey's humanistic naturalism made him strive constantly to bring into rational focus the so-called subjective values of aesthetics, religion and ethics and give them honorable partnership with the presumed objective values of science. When the consciousness of science is fully impregnated with the consciousness of human value, Dewey wrote in a typical summary statement, "the greatest dualism which now weighs humanity down, the split between the material, the mechanical, the scientific and the moral and ideal will be destroyed."

As we pointed out, all the strands of Dewey's thinking converge toward a central preoccupation with experience. He thought of it as the category most likely to underscore "the continuities among subject matters that are always getting split up into dualisms." Experience is defined most succinctly in *Art as Experience* as the interaction between a living organism and its environment. When we think of our experience we think of some connection we have had with something outside of ourselves: a good meal, a warm friendship, a refreshing hike in the mountains. In this broad sense, experience stands for all transactions between man and nature—from the limited, most simple forms of organic behavior to the complex activity of self-conscious human beings. But because our experiences can abort, because they often tend toward fragmentation and incoherence, Dewey stressed the distinction between the broad kind of experience just described and what he called *an* experience (one of the more fruitful distinctions in the annals of modern philosophy). *An* experience is one which has "run its course," which is integrated and consummated. The distinction emphasizes the difference between satisfaction and frustration, connection and disconnection, the whole rather than the parts. In these *real* experiences, Dewey notes, "every successive part flows freely, without seam and without unfilled blanks, into what ensues. At the same time there is no sacrifice of the self-identity of the parts . . . Because of continuous merging, there are no holes, mechanical junctions and dead centers. There are pauses, places of rest, but they punctuate and define the quality of the movement. They sum up what has been undergone and prevent its dissipation and idle evaporation."[10] These are the integral experiences that are genuinely worthwhile, truly enriching. In a word, they are aesthetic.

The prototype for aesthetic experience is always for Dewey in the first instance biological. In this he is much like Marx. He always considered animal activity the symbol of the unity of experience. The live animal, he says, "is fully present, all there, in all of its actions." Animal desire, undistracted by the division of labor or reflexive modes of thought, thrusts directly to its object. Animals have no epistemological problems. Unlike man, they are not haunted by memories from the past; nor are they in dread of the future or racked by guilt. They share more directly in the wholeness of nature.

> When despair for the world grows in me
> and I wake in the night at the least sound
> in fear of what my life and my children's
> > lives may be,
> I go and lie down where the wood drake
> rests in his beauty on the water, and the
> > great heron feeds.
> I come into the peace of wild things
> who do not tax their lives with forethought
> of grief. I come into the presence of still water.
> And I feel above me the day-blind stars
> Waiting with their light. For a time
> I rest in the grace of the world and am free.

Wendell Berry's poem admirably captures Dewey's understanding of experience as a sharing in the "heightened vitality" of nature's rhythms, as a consummatory penetration of the self into the world of objects and events. Experience, then, is not something that goes on exclusively within consciousness, bearing only indirect relations to its world. We tend conventionally, Dewey said, to think in ways that favor dualisms. We spontaneously imagine experience as "an uneasy joining of paired opposites." But this is not the way it need be at all. By placing all modes of experience within nature and viewing them as processes characterized by organic coordination, Dewey hoped to avoid the dichotomy that has been perpetrated by our major disciplines. The core of Dewey's theory of experience is thus the linkage of the self with its world. When this is broken, then the various ways in which the self interacts with that world lose their organic character. Well might he write: "Whenever the bond that binds the living creature to his environment is broken, there is nothing that holds together the various phases and factors of the self. Thought, emotion, sense, purpose, impulsion fall apart and are assigned to different compartments of our being. For their unity is found in the co-operative roles they play in active and receptive relations to the environment."[11]

What animals do by instinct man must achieve by intelligence, particularly intelligence under the aegis of the imagination. Dealienation is basically a matter of unifying, of connecting up the scattered fragments of our experience. And this work of connection is essentially a matter of creativity, which is to say the work of intelligence functioning imaginatively. The imagination is man's connective as well as his creative faculty. This is to say that man must create his meanings; the kind of link between self and world we are talking about is not something given; nor is it something discovered; it is literally something made. When we talk about meaninglessness today we are talking about this loss of imaginative control over our lives, the inability to create meanings. The turmoil of our times reflects this loss and bespeaks the need for controlling metaphors, a master insight by means of which the materials of experience may be symbolically transformed. In modern times it has become more and more the task of the artist to so order experience. "To erupt into reality, and thereby create our connections, becomes the task of the work of art," as Louis Kampf put it. This may at first seem like too heavy a burden to place upon the artist's shoulders. After all, isn't it the work of philosophers and religions to create meaning? Not at all. This is one of the assumptions that inevitably lead to a polarization of experience. The larger point that must be stressed here is this: It is not only the artist who must create. It is man himself.

Thus does he maximize his being. This "fictional" dimension of human meaning must be taken as a fact in any science of man. It is as much part of him as his biology. This, of course, sets a problem: meanings must be created in reference to man's biological roots in the nature of things. Otherwise we face a dual pitfall. Either the meanings we create will be romantic and unreferential (Quixote) or we fall prey to a naturalistic determinism. In either case life is depreciated and experience is fragmented. In brief, the problem of the establishment of meaning through aesthetic reconstruction is how to integrate man's symbolic nature with his biological nature. As Becker put it succinctly, *homo poeta* has to resolve the problem of the separateness and fragility of his own created meanings against the hard backdrop of organisms and objects provided by brute nature. Aesthetic experience may be taken as a prototype for two quite obvious reasons. First of all, art is a unifying medium; it weds dualism and heals dichotomies—appearance and essence, meaning and reality, content and form, spirit and matter, or whatever. Secondly, the artist is one who knows what the possibilities of materiality are; he can discern ideal possibilities in the most unpromising elements of experience. The artist tells us that we do not really see things until we see them imaginatively perfected. This is the message as well of the philosopher and the saint. Ideality is a process at work in the imaginative experience of men. It has been noted of Plato that he viewed the good life as an artist, trying to discern what he could of human possibilities in it, what might be created from the given human materials. This is "an affair of imaginative vision. Knowledge is taken to be what the artist's imagination perceives, the possibilities resident in his materials . . . Philosophy is experience clarified and made whole by the spirit of man —of man the artist."[12] The meanings thus created constitute a superordinate category of experience by which man merges himself in the world, achieves high conviction and defeats the meaninglessness of dumb desire and brute nature (Goethe). Spirit, to revert to Hegel's language, must be at home in the marketplace of concrete reality. It cannot negate its sensual media but must have intercourse with the world. It is through aesthetic transformation that meanings are imposed on the material stuff of the given.*

Alienation and Revolution

I do not want to give the impression that aesthetic transformation is a mere mental attitude, something purely abstract. Quite the contrary. The transformation I speak

* We must bear in mind, of course, the contemporary artist's tarnished self-image. He too is alienated, bound to the wheel of destiny. He too is caught in the snares of many worlds half lost and half found. Professor Anton offers a helpful historical *aperçu* on the artist's dilemma: "The Industrial Revolution crowned and confirmed the secular stratification of modern institutions. The Romantic hero is in a genuine way the expres-

of includes as an intrinsic element the reshaping of the socio-political realm in light of ideals imaginatively discerned. That is why an effective aesthetic must always be revolutionary: it aims at the improvement of the conditions under which men live.* This is another way of saying that there can be no overcoming of alienation without some form of revolution. The latter answers to felt needs, to the gaps in experience; it heals the dichotomies of existence in the concrete. That is why an age of alienation such as our own is also an age of revolution. In fact, we may state further that the revolutionary spirit, with its hope of greater freedom and a new order of things, is unprecedented in our day. The thrust of this spirit is to fuse ideas and experience, to expand the sense of the self and create a society in which that self might survive. The aspiration is, as Trotsky put

---

sion of the artist's self image summoned to oppose the formidable organizations of institutionalized power. The artist, hardly equipped for a sustained competition, became increasingly lonely and was forced to develop a bifocal vision: he had to keep one eye on his artistic concepts and the other on earning his livelihood by peddling his works to the public. As the gap between his two concerns widened, the artist frequently resorted to cultural prophecies and social castigations like those of Hölderlin, Carlyle, Flaubert, Wordsworth, Coleridge, Shelley, Whitman, and Nietzsche, to mention only a few writers. It was Nietzsche who summed up the Romantic reaction-image, advocating its conversion into one of radical action and defiance. After Nietzsche, the artist's image had to face its inherent dilemma: to choose between the illusion of cultural glory or to accept the consequences of its subjectivism. With the advent of Freud's discoveries, the second alternative was made at once palatable and promising. Herein lie the beginnings of the contemporary self image of the artist." (See John Anton, "The One and the Many: The Changing Roles of the Artist," *The Minnesota Review*, Vol. V (1965), p. 179.)

*This position is diametrically opposed to the Marxist theory that communism will signal the end of economics and the advent of aesthetics, a time of free and creative activity. This artificial divorce between the social and the aesthetic betrays Marx's idealism and renders his formula for the "transcendence of human self-alienation" a largely utopian one. The aesthetic attitude is a *sine-qua-non* condition of social reform, not a consequence of it.

it, to impregnate the forms of existence with dramatic dynamism.

Let me elaborate upon this by pointing to three prevalent attitudes toward revolution which I believe to be false precisely because they would deny it as an effective agent of dealienation. The first and most obvious is that revolution is per se undesirable and everything must be done to prevent it. This attitude amounts to a defense of the status quo. In our culture the perspective common to the majority of the people is defined by the analytic, pragmatic values of a dominant and dominating technocratic order. To question this order never occurs to large numbers. It is assumed that its stunning mastery of the natural environment will be extended to the social order in due course by a process of harmonious and gradual adaptation. For such people this order represents *the* rational way of doing things; it is thought to be inevitably in the service of greater economic well-being and moral growth. They assume, as Richard Schaull writes, that "life moves upward in spirals, that the lot of the dispossessed world can be improved without fundamentally upsetting our position in it, and that the values and patterns of life which we have labored long to develop will sooner or later be accepted and appreciated by the rest of the world." Clearly, such an attitude must reject any thought of revolution as either desirable or possible. As a consequence, the great enslavement and alienation imposed by any uncritically accepted system goes largely unnoticed and unchallenged. Thus desensitized, we lose our critical powers and mistake slavery for freedom, the irrational for rationality and the desired for the desirable. Not unsurprisingly this kind of social and political rigidity sooner or later invites its own overthrow. The natural force of social dynamics in the end breaks through such unthinking resistance to lay the groundwork for a new beginning, a *novus ordo saeculorum*. Unfortunately the price paid in violence and bloodshed is usually great.

A second erroneous conception of revolution holds that now and again social conditions justify a revolution but only as a last resort, a kind of sporadic effort that is in the final analysis justified by the stable order it envisages. What is important to this view is more the intended outcome of the revolution rather than the revolutionary initiative as such. For example, the Declaration of Independence explains some of the conditions that legitimize revolution. Yet ironically the main sweep of the history of the United States since that time has been profoundly non-revolutionary, so much so that today the country is bent indefatigably toward conformity. This is all the more ironical in that there are conditions in American society now that more convincingly call for revolutionary action than those which justified the original break with England. This fallacy characterizes all utopian thinking—Marxist, Christian, or whatever. The assumption is that a time will come when there will be no cause for revolution, when a heaven on earth will have been effectively realized—whether in the form of a classless society or the peaceful co-existence of lamb and lion or the accession of philosopher kings.

This attitude denies the ongoing, *evolutionary* dimension of revolution and at the same time ignores a fundamental law of biological and moral growth. Radical cultural mutations are rare and on the whole undesirable. Rather, effective revolution consists in holding the conditions and institutions of society under the progressive scrutiny of critical reason. In this way their shortcomings are more readily perceived; by the same token their strengths can be more effectively utilized. When Socrates was urged by his friends to flee Athens after he had been condemned to death, he refused on the grounds that such a course of action would contradict the basic tenet of his philosophy: namely, that the unexamined life is not worth living. The corollary of this is that the unexamined society is not worth living in. Socrates carried on his dialectic not only with the men of Athens but with the laws and institutions of the state as well. He made an agreement with his state such that he really had only one alternative. "You must do whatever your state and your country tell you to do, or you must persuade them that their commands are unjust," he says in the *Crito*. The emphasis here is on the citizen's critical responsibility. In a democracy the relationship between the citizen and his society is an intrinsic one. In order to change or improve the laws the citizen must work *within* them. The democratic principle is grounded in the fact that the laws hold their authority from the people. Thus, strictly speaking, there is only one way Socrates can appeal his sentence: by persuading his fellow citizens that they have erred in their judgment of him. Since he failed to do so he is logically constrained to abide by the sentence. But it is not just a question of logic. It is also a matter of psychological identity. Socrates is what he is because he is an Athenian. He has become a philosopher, a practitioner of dialectic, because the laws of Athens allowed him to do so. Thus to put himself outside the laws, he would also have to abandon his philosophy. But this would be self-contradictory and compromise his identity. To opt out would be to deny both the democratic principle as well as the social function of critical reason. Thus Socrates saw the condition of freedom as critical alertness. He believed that by the power of reason man can free himself in some significant measure from the evil that exists in his social world. Education in one (but only one) of its important aspects is education for the intelligent critique of society. In a tyranny, of course, it would be permissible to escape it or overthrow it.

But a democracy defines a more creative interaction between citizen and society. Indeed, it defines revolution in terms of this creative interaction, a permanent adaptation of reason to social conditions.*

Unless we see revolution as a form of evolution, a critical exchange between man and his society, we render it a virtually impotent concept. It could mean no more than a static return to the same state of affairs (which, of course, is the original astronomical meaning of the term), the rise and fall of empires in a cyclical, pointless fashion, the replacement of one system by another as in a South American coup. But if this be the reality of revolution, it could not be the agent of new beginnings. It could not, in a word, answer to the deep aspirations of modern man. For this reason, I find the traditional definitions of revolution in terms of sudden social upheavals and/or radical transformations in the governmental process misleading when not in fact false. Even those violent outbursts history books have familiarized us with were preceded by evolutionary social and cultural changes. When, for example, Eugene Kamenda writes that "Unless we confine the term 'revolution' to the field of convulsive changes we shall find revolution every-

---

* For an excellent interpretation of the Socratic dialogues along these lines, see Daniel E. Anderson, "Socrates' Concept of Piety," in *Journal of the History of Philosophy* (January, 1967), pp. 1–13. Anderson comments: "Socrates is what he is because of the dialectical relationship that, throughout his life, has existed between himself and the laws of the society in which he lives. He could at any time in his life have established this relationship with another set of laws by moving to another state— but in doing so he would have created a new identity for himself. At this point the dialectic with the laws is secondary to the dialectic that takes place between Socrates and the dialectic itself. This more basic dialectic is more than a voyage of self-discovery. It is an act of self-creation in which the individual arrives at self-knowledge by creating an identity, by creating himself. The major factor in this self-creation is his choice of his partner in the dialectic—particularly his choice of the laws under which he will live" (p. 12).

where, all the time," one understands the perspective from which he writes but wonders why he is reluctant to accept revolution as an ongoing affair. Or this statement by Chalmers Johnson: "Creative political action is the specific antidote to revolutionary conditions." My point is rather that creative political action *is* revolutionary. When social structures are flexible enough to answer to new needs and respond to the intimations of reason and imagination they foster the kind of revolution that is the very substance of a democratic community.

Finally, there is no need to assume that revolution must always be accompanied by violence. Given the facts of human nature as we know them, the future of violence in some form or other is relatively safe. But the sense of revolution I urge would have as one of its happiest effects the reduction of violence. I have in mind something like what Camus meant by rebellion, and perhaps I can make my meaning clearer by commenting further on the important distinction explained in *The Rebel* between rebellion and revolution (always understood as violent revolution). Camus observed that the course of revolution from Rousseau to Stalin has led inevitably to a reinforcement of state power, usually in the form of authoritarian dictatorship. Camus saw clearly the nihilistic base of modern revolutions which always end in a contempt for man and in mass murder. Revolutionaries, Camus noted, begin by demanding justice and end by establishing a police force. Thus the Jacobins prepared the terror in the name of Liberty; Khrushchev invaded Hungary in the name of History; and we can all think of crimes that have been committed in the name of Democracy. The revolutionary is inspired by abstractions and led to excess, to a going beyond due measure. The rebel on the other hand places integrity and the needs of individual persons above abstractions. To rebel is to say no to a certain state of affairs that violates our moral sense; but it is also to say yes to a desirable state of affairs, to affirm a human value and not merely an abstract one. Rebellion is always based upon the principle of limitation. The revolutionary is an ideologue; he wants wholesale reform and strives to abolish evil. The rebel is more realistic; he strives for partial reforms and limited victories over the universal sense of evil. The revolutionary believes that a utopia is possible; the rebel hopes only to create the conditions of a more livable life. Camus stated the distinction well when he said that we have to choose between "Nordic intemperance and Mediterranean moderation, between eternally adolescent violence and mature strength, between nostalgia (aggravated by learning and books) and courage tempered and enlightened by experience of life. In short, between history and nature."

In *The Rebel* Camus proposed "to face the reality of the present, which is logical crime, and to examine meticulously the arguments by which it is justified; it is an attempt to understand the times in which we live. One might think that a period which, in a space of fifty years, uproots, enslaves, or kills seventy million human beings should be condemned out of hand. But its culpability must still be understood . . . It is incumbent upon us to give a definite answer to the question implicit in the blood and strife of this century." Camus went on to argue that the cause of historical revolution during the past two centuries is a romantic quest for totality which has resulted in despotic and apocalyptic ideologies. In rebelling against the old absolutism (e.g. the divine right of kings) the revolutionaries substituted a new absolutism. Starting from the premise of unlimited freedom they arrived (not illogically) at unlimited despotism. It is this unlimited character of revolutions, one might almost say their wantonness, that Camus consistently deplores. He seems to me profoundly right when he says that the principle of all revolutions is that human nature is infinitely malleable or, what comes to the same thing, that there is no human nature.

> Absolute revolution, in fact, supposes the absolute malleability of human nature and its possible reduction to the condition of a historical force. But rebellion, in man, is the refusal to be treated as an object and to be reduced to simple historical terms. It is the affirmation of a nature common to all men, which eludes the world of power . . . Man, by rebelling, imposes in his turn a limit to history, and at this limit the promise of a value is born. It is the birth of this value that the Caesarean revolution implacably combats because it presages its final defeat . . . [p. 250].

Camus postulates a human nature with an accompanying value pattern as an answer to the blood-letting madness of modern history. In harking back to the Hellenic emphasis on limit and moderation, he takes his stand against those who make absolute claims for freedom. Both Christianity and Marxism, in Camus' view, "postpone to a point beyond the span of history the cure of evil and murder, which are nevertheless experienced within the span of history." Man is a relative creature; he should have learned by now that to taste of the fruit of Absolutism is to poison the wells of human creativity and prepare the path of nihilism. Camus urges us to relearn that the first condition of being a man is to refuse to be a god. This philosophy of finiteness seems to me an excellent guiding principle for the kind of revolution needed today. It would, I believe, protect us against the romantic *putschism* that on all sides postures as revolution. Man is not made for history or any other abstraction. The center of moral gravity lies along the horizon of his creative powers. Let me say, in conclusion, that some new combination of art and politics would be a most desirable form of creativity today.

---

1. Marcus Klein, *After Alienation: American Novels in Mid-Century* (New York, Meridian, 1962).
2. Ernest Becker, *Beyond Alienation: A Philosophy of Education for the Crisis of Democracy* (New York, Braziller, 1967).
3. Russell Baker, "All the Facts About Progress," *New York Times News Service*, 1970.
4. See further developments in Northrop Frye, *The Modern Century* (New York, Oxford, 1967), pp. 34 ff.
5. Stanley Rosen, *Nihilism: A Philosophical Essay* (New Haven, Yale University Press, 1969), p. xv.
6. Earl Rovit, "On the Contemporary Apocalyptic Imagination," *The American Scholar*, November, 1968.
7. A. N. Whitehead, *Process and Reality* (New York, Harper Torchbooks, 1957), p. 4.
8. William James, *The Writings of William James—A Comprehensive Edition*, edited by John McDermott (New York, Random House, 1967), p. 314.
9. John Dewey, "From Absolutism to Experimentalism," in *John Dewey: On Experience, Nature, and Freedom*, edited by Richard Bernstein (New York, The Library of Liberal Arts, 1960), pp. 10–11.
In his early idealist phase Dewey thought of experience in terms of an organic oneness, a kind of seamless garment without breaks or splits. Later he became critical of this interpretation. First of all, he distrusted the cognitive bias of idealism, its tendency to reduce all experience to a form of knowing. This was to pay too dearly for unity. He gave preference to things *had* over things *cognized*, noting that they are "objects to be treated, used, acted upon and with, enjoyed and endured, even

more than things to be known." Secondly, Dewey drifted more toward a pluralism which recognized the independence as well as the inter-relatedness of situations, contexts, and events. This was in keeping with his naturalism and his conviction that the unity of experience derives from a biological basis rather than an idealist construct.

10. John Dewey, *Art as Experience* (New York, Capricorn Books, 1934), p. 36.

11. *Ibid.*, p. 252. Dewey speaks most convincingly about the unity of experience when he has biological and aesthetic models in mind. He is less convincing, it seems to me, when he favors scientific thinking as a model for philosophy, even though his view of scientific method was never a narrowly positivistic one. This is one of the unresolved tensions in Dewey's theory of experience.

12. J. H. Randall, *Plato: Dramatist of the Life of Reason* (New York, Columbia University Press, 1970), p. 137.

Index

□ INDEX

□ INDEX

□ INDEX

☐ INDEX

About the Author

BERNARD MURCHLAND is professor of philosophy at Ohio Wesleyan University. He received his Ph.D. from the State University of New York at Buffalo. He has edited *The Meaning of the Death of God* and *Two Views of Man,* and written for *Commonweal, worldview, The New Republic, The Wall Street Journal,* and many scholarly journals.